INTRODUCING
ISSUES WITH
OPPOSING
VIEWPOINTS®

Poverty

Mike Wilson, *Book Editor*

GREENHAVEN PRESS
A part of Gale, Cengage Learning

GALE
CENGAGE Learning™

Detroit • New York • San Francisco • New Haven, Conn • Waterville, Maine • London

Christine Nasso, *Publisher*
Elizabeth Des Chenes, *Managing Editor*

LIBRARY OF CONGRESS CATALOGING-IN-PUBLICATION DATA

Poverty / Mike Wilson, book editor.
    p. cm. -- (Introducing issues with opposing viewpoints)
 Includes bibliographical references and index.
 ISBN 978-0-7377-4340-1 (hardcover)
1. Poverty. I. Wilson, Mike, 1954-
HC79.P6P677 2009
362.5--dc22

2008055847

Printed in the United States of America
1 2 3 4 5 6 7 13 12 11 10 09

Contents

Foreword

Indulging in a wide spectrum of ideas, beliefs, and perspectives is a critical cornerstone of democracy. After all, it is often debates over differences of opinion, such as whether to legalize abortion, how to treat prisoners, or when to enact the death penalty, that shape our society and drive it forward. Such diversity of thought is frequently regarded as the hallmark of a healthy and civilized culture. As the Reverend Clifford Schutjer of the First Congregational Church in Mansfield, Ohio, declared in a 2001 sermon, "Surrounding oneself with only like-minded people, restricting what we listen to or read only to what we find agreeable is irresponsible. Refusing to entertain doubts once we make up our minds is a subtle but deadly form of arrogance." With this advice in mind, Introducing Issues with Opposing Viewpoints books aim to open readers' minds to the critically divergent views that comprise our world's most important debates.

Introducing Issues with Opposing Viewpoints simplifies for students the enormous and often overwhelming mass of material now available via print and electronic media. Collected in every volume is an array of opinions that captures the essence of a particular controversy or topic. Introducing Issues with Opposing Viewpoints books embody the spirit of nineteenth-century journalist Charles A. Dana's axiom: "Fight for your opinions, but do not believe that they contain the whole truth, or the only truth." Absorbing such contrasting opinions teaches students to analyze the strength of an argument and compare it to its opposition. From this process readers can inform and strengthen their own opinions, or be exposed to new information that will change their minds. Introducing Issues with Opposing Viewpoints is a mosaic of different voices. The authors are statesmen, pundits, academics, journalists, corporations, and ordinary people who have felt compelled to share their experiences and ideas in a public forum. Their words have been collected from newspapers, journals, books, speeches, interviews, and the Internet, the fastest growing body of opinionated material in the world.

Introducing Issues with Opposing Viewpoints shares many of the well-known features of its critically acclaimed parent series, Opposing Viewpoints. The articles are presented in a pro/con format, allowing readers to absorb divergent perspectives side by side. Active reading questions preface each viewpoint, requiring the student to approach the material thoughtfully and carefully. Useful charts, graphs, and cartoons supplement each article. A thorough introduction provides readers with crucial background on an issue. An annotated bibliography points the reader toward articles, books, and Web sites that contain additional information on the topic. An appendix of organizations to contact contains a wide variety of charities, nonprofit organizations, political groups, and private enterprises that each hold a position on the issue at hand. Finally, a comprehensive index allows readers to locate content quickly and efficiently.

Introducing Issues with Opposing Viewpoints is also significantly different from Opposing Viewpoints. As the series title implies, its presentation will help introduce students to the concept of opposing viewpoints and learn to use this material to aid in critical writing and debate. The series' four-color, accessible format makes the books attractive and inviting to readers of all levels. In addition, each viewpoint has been carefully edited to maximize a reader's understanding of the content. Short but thorough viewpoints capture the essence of an argument. A substantial, thought-provoking essay question placed at the end of each viewpoint asks the student to further investigate the issues raised in the viewpoint, compare and contrast two authors' arguments, or consider how one might go about forming an opinion on the topic at hand. Each viewpoint contains sidebars that include at-a-glance information and handy statistics. A Facts About section located in the back of the book further supplies students with relevant facts and figures.

Following in the tradition of the Opposing Viewpoints series, Greenhaven Press continues to provide readers with invaluable exposure to the controversial issues that shape our world. As John Stuart Mill once wrote: "The only way in which a human being can make some approach to knowing the whole of a subject is by hearing what can be said about it by persons of every variety of opinion and studying all modes in which it can be looked at by every character of mind. No wise man ever acquired his wisdom in any mode but this." It is to this principle that Introducing Issues with Opposing Viewpoints books are dedicated.

Introduction

"The fact is that this generation—yours, my generation . . . we're the first generation that can look at poverty and disease, look across the ocean to Africa and say with a straight face, we can be the first to end this sort of stupid extreme poverty, where in the world of plenty, a child can die for lack of food in its belly."

  —Bono, University of Pennsylvania 2004 Commencement Address

"Any strategy to reduce intergenerational poverty has to be centered on work, not welfare—not only because work provides independence and income but also because work provides order, structure, dignity, and opportunities for growth in people's lives."

                        —Barack Obama, *The Audacity of Hope*

"Inequality undermines our culture and civic life, breaking down the social cohesion and solidarity required for healthy communities."

                        —Chuck Collins, Institute for Policy Studies

What is poverty? The three quotes appearing above all are about property but look at poverty in different ways. The first characterizes poverty as deprivation—unmet basic human needs. The second references meaningful participation in society, or social inclusion. The third considers poverty in terms of relative inequality.

Ireland's Office of Social Inclusion (OSI) defines poverty as "deprivation due to a lack of resources, both material and non-material, e.g. income, housing, health, education, knowledge and culture. It requires a threshold to measure it." This is the aspect of poverty to which rock singer Bono refers in the quote above. According to the United Nations, 90 percent of the world's hungry "live with chronic hunger—a nagging hunger that does not go away." When authors writing about poverty use terms such as "extreme poverty," they usually are referring to those deprived of the necessities of life.

The United Nations seeks to end extreme poverty by the year 2015. In the year 2000, 189 world leaders met at the UN Millennium Summit and signed the Millennium Declaration, agreeing to meet "Millennium Development Goals" (MDGs). The MDGs constitute a plan with measurable goals and deadlines for reducing poverty and are discussed in some of the viewpoints in this volume.

Another aspect of poverty is social exclusion. OSI defines social exclusion as "being unable to participate in society because of a lack of resources that are normally available to the general population. It can refer to both individuals, and communities in a broader framework, with linked problems such as low incomes, poor housing, high crime environments and family problems."

Meaningful participation in the social and economic structures of society, alluded to in the quote by Barack Obama, is part of social inclusion. According to statements by the European Union, the EU's program to help eradicate poverty by 2010 makes "implementation of ambitious and effective policies on social inclusion . . . a priority for the European Union." In order to have social cohesion necessary for healthy communities, everyone must have meaningful participation and be "stakeholders" in society. Economic modernization, in the view of the European Union, "must go hand in hand with promoting social cohesion and, in particular, with an open method of coordination designed to prevent and eradicate poverty and exclusion." In this view, eradicating poverty and exclusion caused by poverty helps create the social cohesion needed for a healthy society. The focus is not just on individual deprivation but the harm poverty causes all of us by dividing our society into "haves" and "have-nots."

The third quote above says inequality of wealth also harms social cohesion. But is inequality truly an aspect of poverty? OSI calls inequality "a comparative or relative concept. It does not measure deprivation or poverty and does not require a threshold. It is possible for inequality to exist with or without poverty. Similarly, poverty can exist with or without inequality."

A 2006 report from the Inter-American Development Bank (IDB) illustrates this point. The report found that the average salary of those newly arrived to the United States from Latin America was less than two-thirds of U.S. government poverty-level income for a family of four. But the IDB report also found that immigrants will send home approximately $45 billion in remittances in 2006, creating "one of the broadest and most effective poverty alleviation programs in the world." These immigrants were poor relative to most U.S. families but wealthy relative to families in their country of origin.

Yet too much inequality of wealth, many argue, is harmful. Future Supreme Court Justice Louis Brandeis, commenting on extremes of wealth during the late 19th century, stated, "We can have a democratic society or we can have great concentrated wealth in the hands of a few. We cannot have both." Chuck Collins, an analyst for the Institute for Policy Studies, observes that "the evidence that inequality does matter has been steadily mounting. The corrosive and growing concentration of wealth and power sits at the root of many of our most urgent societal problems. Extreme inequality is bad for our democracy, bad for our culture, and bad for our economy." Others take issue with this point of view, arguing that inequality is irrelevant if everyone has the ability to meet basic human needs such as food and shelter.

As you read the viewpoints in this volume—*Introducing Issues with Opposing Viewpoints: Poverty*—keep in mind the three aspects of poverty: deprivation, social exclusion, and inequality of wealth. Whether an author defines poverty to include all three, or to include only deprivation, affects an author's view of the degree to which poverty is a problem and the measures needed to address the problem. Differences in definitions of poverty can account for why one author is accused of exaggerating the problem and another is accused of heartless indifference.

Chapter 1

Is Poverty a Problem?

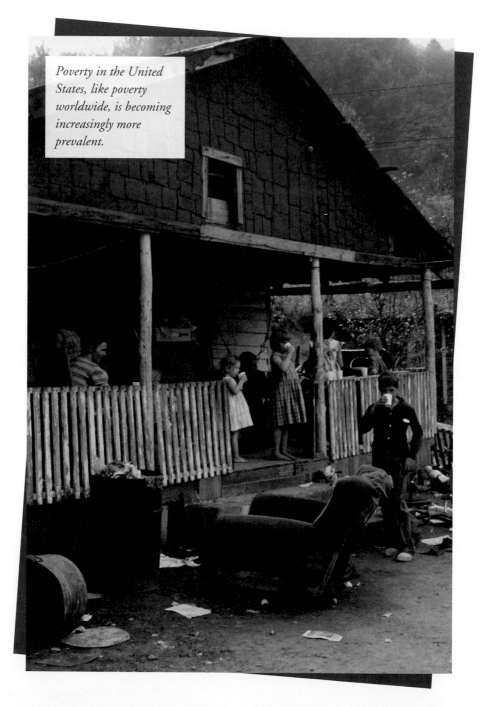

Poverty in the United States, like poverty worldwide, is becoming increasingly more prevalent.

Viewpoint

1

Worldwide Poverty Is a Serious Problem

Jeffrey D. Sachs

"A large number of the extreme poor are caught in a poverty trap, unable on their own to escape from extreme material deprivation."

Jeffrey D. Sachs argues in this viewpoint that poverty is a serious problem. The author divides the world into different "rungs" on an economic ladder but says that many in the world are not even on the ladder. Geography, corrupt governments, cultural norms, and even poverty itself, he argues, create conditions that result in 40 percent of the world's population being poor or extremely poor. Sachs is the director of the Earth Institute at Columbia University and special adviser to the United Nations on Millennium Development Goals.

AS YOU READ, CONSIDER THE FOLLOWING QUESTIONS:
1. According to the author, how many persons in the world are extremely poor?
2. What percentage of the world is experiencing economic progress, according to Sachs?
3. In the author's view, what is the main reason the poorest of the poor are trapped by their own poverty?

Jeffrey D. Sachs, "Ending Poverty in Our Time," *Human Rights,* vol. 32, July 1, 2005, pp. 17–21.

I f economic development is a ladder with higher rungs representing steps up the path to economic well-being, there are roughly 1 billion people around the world, one-sixth of humanity, who live as the Malawians do: too ill, hungry, or destitute even to get a foot on the first rung of the development ladder. These people are the "poorest of the poor," or the "extreme poor" of the planet. They all live in developing countries (poverty does exist in rich countries, but it is not extreme poverty). Of course, not all of these one billion people are dying today, but they are all fighting for survival each day. If they are the victims of a serious drought or flood, or an episode of serious illness, or a collapse of the world market price of their cash crop, the result is likely to be extreme suffering and perhaps even death. Cash earnings are pennies a day.

The Development Ladder

A few rungs up the development ladder is the upper end of the low-income world, where roughly another 1.5 billion people face problems like those of the young women in Bangladesh. These people are "the poor." They live above mere subsistence. Although daily survival is pretty much assured, they struggle in the cities and countryside to make ends meet. Death is not at their door, but chronic financial hardship and a lack of basic amenities such as safe drinking water and functioning latrines are part of their daily lives. All told, the extreme poor (at around 1 billion) and the poor (another 1.5 billion) make up around 40 percent of humanity.

Another 2.5 billion people, including the Indian IT [information technology] workers, are up yet another few rungs, in the middle-income world. These are middle-income households, but they would certainly not be recognized as middle class by the standards of rich countries. Their incomes may be a few thousand dollars per year. Most of them live in cities. They are able to secure some comfort in their housing, perhaps even indoor plumbing. They can purchase a scooter and someday even an automobile. They have adequate clothing, and their children go to school. Their nutrition is adequate, and some are even falling into the rich-world syndrome of unhealthy fast food.

Still higher up the ladder are the remaining 1 billion people, roughly one-sixth of the world, in the high-income world. These affluent

Region	% in $1 a day poverty	Population (millions)	Population in $1 a day poverty (millions)
East Asia and Pacific	9.07%	1,885.0	170.0
Latin America and the Caribbean	8.63%	549.0	47.0
South Asia	31.08%	1,470.0	456.0
Sub-Saharan Africa	41.09%	753.0	309.0
Total developing countries			982.0
Europe and Central Asia	0.95%	460.0	1.0
Middle East and North Africa	1.47%	306.0	4.0
Total			987.0

Taken from: World Hunger Education Service, 2008. www.worldhunger.org.

households include the billion or so people in the rich countries, but also the increasing number of affluent people living in middle-income countries—the tens of millions of high-income individuals in such cities as Shanghai, São Paolo, or Mexico City. The young professionals of Beijing are among the fortunate one-sixth of the world enjoying twenty-first-century affluence.

One-Sixth Trapped in Poverty

The good news is that well more than half of the world, from the Bangladesh garment worker onward, broadly speaking, is experiencing economic progress. Not only do they have a foothold on the development ladder, but they are also actually climbing it. Their climb is evident in rising personal incomes and the acquisition of goods such as cell phones, television sets, and scooters. Progress is also evident in such crucial determinants of economic well-being as rising life expectancy, falling infant mortality rates, rising educational attainment, increasing access to water and sanitation, and the like.

The greatest tragedy of our time is that one-sixth of humanity is not even on the development ladder. A large number of the extreme poor are caught in a poverty trap, unable on their own to escape from extreme material deprivation. They are trapped by disease, physical isolation, climate stress, environmental degradation, and by extreme poverty itself. Even though life-saving solutions exist to increase their chances for survival—whether in the form of new farming techniques, or essential medicines, or bed nets that can limit the transmission of malaria—these families and their governments simply lack the financial means to make these crucial investments. The world's poor know about the development ladder: they are tantalized by images of affluence from halfway around the world. But they are not able to get a first foothold on the ladder, and so cannot even begin the climb out of poverty. . . .

The Poverty Trap

The most common explanation for why countries fail to achieve economic growth often focuses on the faults of the poor: poverty is a result of corrupt leadership and retrograde cultures that impede modern development. However, something as complex as a society's economic system has too many moving parts to presume that only one thing can go wrong. Problems can occur in different parts of the economic machine and can sometimes cascade, bringing the machine to a near halt.

The poverty trap: poverty itself as a cause of economic stagnation. The key problem for the poorest countries is that poverty itself can be a trap. When poverty is very extreme, the poor do not have the ability—by themselves—to get out of the mess. Here is why:

Consider the kind of poverty caused by a lack of capital per person. Poor rural villages lack trucks, paved roads, power generators, irrigation channels. Human capital is very low, with hungry, disease-ridden, and illiterate villagers struggling for survival. Natural capital is depleted: the trees have been cut down and the soil nutrients exhausted. In these conditions the need is for more capital—physical, human, natural—but that requires more saving. When people are poor, but not utterly destitute, they may be able to save. When they are utterly destitute, they need their entire income, or more, just to survive. There is no margin of income above survival that can be invested for the future.

This is the main reason why the poorest of the poor are most prone to becoming trapped with low or negative economic growth rates. They are too poor to save for the future and thereby accumulate the capital per person that could pull them out of their current misery. . . .

Geography Can Cause Poverty

Physical geography. Even if the poverty trap is the right diagnosis, it still poses the question of why some impoverished countries are trapped and others are not. The answer often lies in the frequently overlooked problems of physical geography. Americans, for example, believe that they earned their wealth all by themselves. They forget that they inherited a vast continent rich in natural resources, with great soils and ample rainfall, immense navigable rivers, and thousands of miles of coastline with dozens of natural ports that provide a wonderful foundation for sea-based trade.

Other countries are not quite so favored. Many of the world's poorest countries are severely hindered by high transport costs because they are landlocked; situated in high mountain ranges; or lack navigable rivers, long coastlines, or good natural harbors. Culture does not explain the persistence of poverty in Bolivia, Ethiopia, Kyrgyzstan, or Tibet. Look instead to the mountain geography of a landlocked region facing crushing transport costs and economic isolation that stifle almost all forms of modern economic activity. . . .

Other kinds of geographical distress are also at play. Many countries are trapped in arid conditions with low agricultural productivity or vulnerability to prolonged droughts. Most of the tropics have

When poverty is extreme, such as in this Thailand slum, the poor do not have the ability to lift themselves out of poverty without government assistance.

ecological conditions that favor killer diseases like malaria, schistosomiasis, dengue fever, and dozens of others. Sub-Saharan Africa, in particular, has an ideal rainfall, temperature, and mosquito type that makes it the global epicenter of malaria, perhaps the greatest factor in slowing Africa's economic growth throughout history.

Government and Poverty

Fiscal trap. Even when the private economy is not impoverished, the government may lack the resources to pay for the infrastructure on which economic growth depends. Governments are critical to investing in public goods and services like primary health care, roads, power grids, ports, and the like. The government may lack the financial means to provide these public goods, however, for at least three reasons. First, the population itself may be impoverished, so taxation of the population is not feasible. Second, the government may be inept, corrupt, or incapacitated, and thereby unable to collect tax revenues. Third, the government may already be carrying a tremendous load of debt (for example, debt carried forward from an earlier decade), and must use its limited tax revenue to service the debt rather than to finance new investments.

Governance failures. Economic development requires a government oriented toward development. The government has many roles to play. It must identify and finance the high-priority infrastructure projects, and make the needed infrastructure and social services available to the whole population, not just a select few. The government must create an environment conducive to investments by private businesses. Those investors must believe that they will be allowed to operate their business and to keep their future profits. Governments must exercise self-restraint in demanding bribes or side payments. Governments must also maintain internal peace and safety so the safety of persons and property is not unduly threatened, maintain judicial systems that can define property rights and honestly enforce contracts, and defend the national territory to keep it safe from invasion.

When governments fail in any of these tasks—leaving huge gaps in infrastructure, or raising corruption to levels that impair economic activity, or failing to ensure domestic peace—the economy is sure to fail, and often to fail badly. Indeed in extreme cases, when governments are unable to perform their most basic functions, we talk about "state failures," which are characterized by wars, revolutions, coups, anarchy, and the like.

Cultural Factors

Cultural barriers. Even when governments are trying to advance their countries, the cultural environment may be an obstacle to development. Cultural or religious norms in the society may block the role of women, for example, leaving half of the population without economic or political rights and without education, thereby undermining half of the population in its contribution to overall development. Denying women their rights and education results in cascading problems. Most important, perhaps, the demographic transition from high fertility to low fertility is delayed or blocked altogether. Poor households continue to have six or seven children because the woman's role is seen mainly as child rearing, and her lack of education means that she has few options in the labor force. In these settings women often lack basic economic security and legal rights; when they are widowed their social circumstances turn even more dreadful, and they are left completely impoverished without hope for improvement.

Similar cultural barriers may apply to religious or ethnic minorities. Social norms may prevent certain groups from gaining access to public services (such as schooling, health facilities, or job training). These minorities may be blocked from entering universities or public sector jobs. They may face harassment in the community, including boycotts of their businesses and physical destruction of property. In extreme circumstances, as occurred in East Africa with the Indian community, wholesale "ethnic cleansing" may ensue, with many fleeing for their lives.

Geopolitics. It takes two to trade. Trade barriers created by foreign countries can impede a poor country's economic development. These barriers are sometimes political, as when a powerful country imposes trade sanctions on a regime that it does not like. These sanctions may aim to weaken or topple a despicable regime, but often they simply impoverish the population of the targeted country without toppling the regime. Many factors in addition to trade that may affect a country's development can be manipulated from abroad for geopolitical reasons.

Lack of innovation. Consider the plight of inventors in an impoverished country. Even if these inventors are able to develop new scientific approaches to meet local economic needs, the chances of recouping investments in research and development through later sales in the local market are very low. The local purchasing power to buy a new product is tiny, and will not provide for sufficient profits if an invention is successfully brought to market, even if the impoverished country has state-of-the-art patent legislation. The problem is not the property rights to the invention, but the size of the market.

The demographic trap. One reason for a poverty trap is a demographic trap, when impoverished families choose to have lots of children. These choices are understandable, yet the results can be disastrous. When impoverished families have large numbers of children, the families cannot afford to invest in the nutrition, health, and education of each child. They might only afford the education of one child, and may send only one son to school. High fertility rates in one generation, therefore, tend to lead to impoverishment of the children and to high fertility rates in the following generation as well. Rapid population growth also puts enormous stresses on farm sizes and environmental resources, thereby exacerbating the poverty.

Poverty Must Be Taken Seriously

Ending global poverty by 2025 will require concerted actions by the rich countries as well as the poor, beginning with a "global compact" between the rich countries and poor countries. The poor countries must take ending poverty seriously, and will have to devote a greater share of their national resources to cutting poverty rather than to war, corruption, and political infighting. The rich countries will need to move beyond the platitudes of helping the poor, and follow through on their repeated promises to deliver more help.

EVALUATING THE AUTHOR'S ARGUMENTS:

How does the author define "poor" and "extremely poor"? Do you agree with his definitions? Why or why not?

Poverty in America Is Overstated

Robert Rector

"Some material hardship does exist in America, but it is quite limited in severity and scope."

Robert Rector argues in this viewpoint that poverty is not a serious problem. Those classified as "poor" by the government, he contends, are actually quite comfortable and own many of the same amenities of life that the middle class have. The author says that poor children in America are not under-nourished, and poor families have more living space than do average citizens living in Europe. Poverty that does exist, he argues, is self-inflicted, and illegal immigration inflates the number of people classified as poor. Rector is senior research fellow in domestic policy studies at the Heritage Foundation.

AS YOU READ, CONSIDER THE FOLLOWING QUESTIONS:

1. According to data cited by the author, how many color TVs does the typical "poor" person have?
2. How does the consumption of protein, vitamins, and minerals by poor children compare to that by middle-class children, according to the author?
3. According to Rector, how many hours per week of work support the typical poor family with children?

The Census Bureau announced [on August 28, 2007] that 36.5 million Americans are "poor." Presidential candidate John Edwards claims these 36.5 million Americans "do not have enough money for the food, shelter and clothing they need." According to Edwards, poverty is an appalling national "plague" forcing "one in eight of us" to live in "terrible" circumstances.

But, if poverty means (as Edwards claims) a lack of nutritious food, adequate warm housing and clothing, then very few of the 36.5 million people identified as "poor" by Census are, in fact, poor.

Some material hardship does exist in America, but it is quite limited in severity and scope.

Poor Are Well Off

According to the government's own data, the typical person defined as "poor" by the Census has cable or satellite TV, air conditioning, a microwave, a DVD player or VCR, and two color TVs. Three quarters of these "poor" own a car and nearly a third have two or more cars.

By his own testimony, the typical "poor" person consistently has enough food to feed his family and enough money to meet all essential expenses such as mortgage, rent, utilities and important medical care. When asked, he reports that his family was able to obtain medical care whenever needed during the past year.

Government data show that 43 percent of all "poor" Americans actually own their own homes—typically, a three-bedroom house with one-and-a-half baths, a garage and a porch or patio.

Only 6 percent of "poor" families are overcrowded. In fact, poor Americans living in houses or apartments, on average, have more living space per person than does the average citizen living in European countries such as England, France and Germany. (Note: this comparison is to the average European, not *poor* Europeans.)

Poor Are Not Hungry

As a group, America's poor are far from chronically undernourished. The average consumption of protein, vitamins and minerals is virtually the same for poor and middle-class children and, in most cases,

Decline in Poverty in the United States from 1959 to 2006

Year	Percent of individuals living in poverty	Year	Percent of individuals living in poverty
2006	12.3%	1982	15.0%
2005	12.6%	1981	14.0%
2004	12.7%	1980	13.0%
2003	12.5%	1979	11.7%
2002	12.1%	1978	11.4%
2001	11.7%	1977	11.6%
2000	11.3%	1976	11.8%
1999	11.9%	1975	12.3%
1998	12.7%	1974	11.2%
1997	13.3%	1973	11.1%
1996	13.7%	1972	11.9%
1995	13.8%	1971	12.5%
1994	14.5%	1970	12.6%
1993	15.1%	1969	12.1%
1992	14.8%	1968	12.8%
1991	14.2%	1967	14.2%
1990	13.5%	1966	14.7%
1989	12.8%	1965	17.3%
1988	13.0%	1964	19.0%
1987	13.4%	1963	19.5%
1986	13.6%	1962	21.0%
1985	14.0%	1961	21.9%
1984	14.4%	1960	22.2%
1983	15.2%	1959	22.4%

Taken from: U.S. Census Bureau. www.census.gov/hhes/www/poverty/histopov/hstpov2.html.

is well above recommended norms. Most poor children today are, in fact, super-nourished—growing up to be, on average, one inch taller and 10 pounds heavier than the GIs who stormed the beaches of Normandy in World War II.

Some poor families do experience temporary food shortages, a condition touted as "hunger" by activists. But even this condition is relatively rare: 89 percent of the poor report their families always have "enough" food to eat, while only 2 percent say they "often" do not have enough to eat.

Poverty Is Self-Inflicted

Much of the official poverty that does exist is self-inflicted, a result of poor decisions and self-defeating behaviors. Weak work ethic plays a big role in poverty: In good economic times or bad, the typical poor family with children is supported by only 800 hours of work during a year—16 hours per week.

If work in each family were raised to 2,000 hours per year— the equivalent of one adult working 40 hours a week throughout the year—nearly 75 percent of poor children would be immediately lifted out of official poverty.

Father absence is another major cause of child poverty. Nearly two-thirds of poor children reside in single-parent homes. Another 1.5 million children are born out of wedlock each year. If poor single mothers married the fathers of their children, almost three-quarters would immediately be lifted out of poverty.

> **FAST FACT**
>
> Worldwide, the number of people living in extreme poverty (subsisting on a daily income of less than U.S. $1) fell 18.4 percent between 2000 and 2004.

While work and marriage are reliable ladders out of poverty, the welfare system remains perversely hostile to both. Despite welfare reform, major programs such as food stamps, public housing and Medicaid continue to reward idleness and penalize marriage. If welfare could be turned around to require work and encourage marriage, poverty among children would drop substantially.

The author contends that data on typical American poor people show they have cable or satellite TV, DVD players, and multiple color TVs and that three-quarters of them own cars.

Illegal Immigration Inflates Poverty

Immigration also plays a major role in U.S. poverty. Each year, our nation imports hundreds of thousands of new poor persons. Porous borders encourage some 800,000 illegal aliens a year to enter the nation. And our legal immigration system strongly favors low-skill immigrants over higher-skill immigrants.

As a result, one quarter of all poor persons in the United States are now immigrants or their minor children. An amazing one in 10 of the poor counted by Census is either an illegal alien or the minor child of an illegal.

Immigrants tend to be poor because they are poorly educated; some 60 percent of illegal aliens and a quarter of legal immigrants lack a high-school degree, compared to 12 percent of native-born Americans. As long as the massive flow of poverty-prone persons from foreign countries continues, efforts to reduce poverty in the United States will be far more difficult. Any sound anti-poverty strategy must stop illegal immigration, and increase the skill level of future legal immigrants.

EVALUATING THE AUTHOR'S ARGUMENTS:

The author frequently cites what he says are the circumstances of the "typical" poor person. Does the author define what that means? How might knowing the author's definition affect your view of his argument?

The Extent of Poverty Depends upon Your Definition

Greg Mellen

"The current poverty threshold is little more than a point of reference."

Greg Mellen argues in this viewpoint that there is disagreement about how poverty should be defined. Originally, he contends, poverty was defined with reference to the cost of feeding a family of four and assuming food made up one-third of a family's living expenses, adjusted for changes in the consumer price index. However, he says, some argue that this approach fails to consider societal changes in standards of living, the increased cost of housing, regional differences, noncash payments, and other factors making the definition of poverty controversial and politically charged. Mellen writes for the *Press-Telegram* in Long Beach, California.

AS YOU READ, CONSIDER THE FOLLOWING QUESTIONS:
1. According to the author, what factor does most of Europe take into account when defining poverty that the United States does not?

2. How much federal money is given away annually based upon definitions of poverty, according to the author?
3. A Northwest Area Foundation poll quoted by the author found that nearly two-thirds of Americans say a family needs how much to make ends meet?

S o, what is poverty exactly and where do we draw the line? Should the poverty line be the bare minimum it takes to feed children and house a family, or something that allows families to cover the expenses of the modern age?

About the only thing anyone agrees on is that the current poverty threshold is little more than a point of reference.

Set Income vs. Societal Standard

The 2005 U.S. Census sets poverty at about $20,000 for a family of four. The line is set by counting before-tax earnings and cash benefits (pensions, child support, dividends etc.). Noncash benefits such as food stamps and housing subsidies don't count, nor do Earned Income Tax Credits.

The poverty threshold is a flat sum that doesn't vary for regions with higher housing and living costs, such as California, nor does it consider costs such as day care, transportation or health care.

Some experts say poverty should remain linked to a set income as it is now. Others say it should reflect rises in the societal standard of living, as is done in much of Europe. Still others say health, life expectancy, living conditions and other factors should be considered. Where one sides is often as much a function of politics as mathematics.

"Efforts to change the current measure have been mired in controversy because, in the end, they are based on subjective determination of what it means to be poor in our rich abundant society," wrote Douglas Besharov, of the conservative American Enterprise Institute, and Peter Germanis in a 2004 paper sponsored by the University of Maryland and federal agencies.

The Original Poverty Formulas

So how did we get here? When the poverty line was first introduced, the purpose was to determine whether families would starve.

In 1963–64, Mollie Orshansky, a then 48-year-old government statistician, developed the formula using low-cost Department of Agriculture food plans, which calculated that a family of four could subsist on a food budget of either $2.80 or $3.60 per day ($3,165 or $3,955 per year). That was multiplied by three, based on another government estimate that a family spent a third of its income on food. Just like that, a threshold was born.

At the time, no formal method for counting the poor or definition for poverty existed. Under the formula, 18 percent to 26 percent of families nationally fell below one of the two thresholds.

The poverty number has been adjusted upward each year with rises in the Consumer Price Index, which measures cost of living based on the retail costs of certain goods and services. Otherwise, the threshold has essentially remained unchanged.

The 2005 threshold for a family of four, which is published each year by the U.S. Census, is between $19,806 and $20,474 before taxes. The lower number is for a family with two parents and two children under 18. The larger is for a family of four with one child under 18. The average weighted threshold is $19,971.

Orshansky's poverty formula was adopted in May 1965, a year after President Lyndon Johnson declared his "war on poverty." By 1969, a modified version of Orshansky's threshold was adopted, based on the lower-cost, two food plan.

Orshansky didn't intend her method to be adopted as an official yardstick and acknowledged it would yield a "conservative underestimate" of poverty.

Programs Spend Based on Poverty Definition

As time has passed, despite attacks from all sides, the Orshansky method has held with only minor changes. Some agencies use different measures to set income limits for aid.

The U.S. Department of Health and Human Services uses a simplified version of the threshold, while the Department of Housing and Urban Development uses county median income levels to set its guidelines. However, the Census threshold, or multiples of it, is the most prevalent determinant of benefits to the poor. The Census poverty rate is the one most often cited by the media and is updated annually.

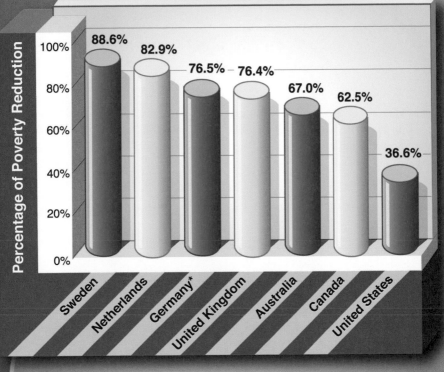

Poverty Reduction After Government Taxes and Income Transfers

Of the countries listed, America has the lowest rate of poverty reduction as a result of specific government programs.

Percentage of Poverty Reduction

- Sweden: 88.6%
- Netherlands: 82.9%
- Germany*: 76.5%
- United Kingdom: 76.4%
- Australia: 67.0%
- Canada: 62.5%
- United States: 36.6%

* Studied only West Germany

Taken from: The Poverty and Democracy Project, "Understanding Poverty," November 3, 2003.
http://condor.depaul.edu/~poverty/understanding_poverty.htm.

Besharov and Germanis found that 12 federal programs spend more than $60 billion annually using the poverty line. It is estimated the United States spends more than $500 billion, or 12 percent of the gross national product, on social aid and relief programs.

Housing Now Costs More than Food

The American society in 2006 is far different from Orshansky's.

In the early 1960s, the main family unit had two parents, one who worked, meaning child care was not a major consideration. In today's

In 1963 Mollie Orshansky developed the formula for measuring the poverty threshold. This formula, with minor changes, is still used today.

world, a family generally spends between one sixth and one seventh of its income on food, rather than one third.

"When I began studying poverty in the 1960s, housing wasn't even in the equation," says Joel Handler, a noted professor and poverty scholar at UCLA. "Now it's the big gorilla in the closet. With people paying 50 percent of their income for housing, they have no money left."

In the past, benefits for the poor were often paid in cash, minimizing noncash benefits as part of the equation. Since 1968, government assistance in cash has fallen from more than 50 percent to less than 20 percent and would be less but for the Earned Income Tax Credit.

Cost of Living Not in Tandem with Income Gains

The only mechanism that changes the poverty line is cost of living. Therefore, it doesn't always rise or fall with societal income gains. In the past five years, despite overall economic gains, poverty has risen four out of five years and was static last year [2006].

This leads liberals to say the poor are left behind when society prospers. Conservatives say projections in the Consumer Price Index are often overestimated, meaning the poverty line is artificially high. There is no method to lower the poverty line.

Today, the threshold of a family of four in poverty is about 36 percent of the national median family income of $55,832 as estimated by the Census. Orshansky's threshold was roughly half the median income.

Regional Differences

To account for societal changes since the threshold was set, several studies have tried to set more realistic thresholds. Several, especially those that look at regional costs of living, have set thresholds to live without government assistance at up to three times poverty.

> **FAST FACT**
>
> The percentage of Mexicans living below the poverty level is 13.8 percent using a food-based definition of poverty but more than 40 percent using an asset-based definition of poverty.

In March [2006], the Northwest Area Foundation poll found that nearly two-thirds of Americans say a family needs $40,000 a year to make ends meet.

When the National Research Council studied poverty in 1995, it found 10 studies that set alternate poverty thresholds, all at higher rates. The threshold at the time was $14,228 for a family of four. Alternate thresholds ranged from a low of $17,200 to $21,800.

Should Noncash Payments Lower Thresholds?

There are some who attack the poverty line for not considering noncash payments. A study by the Census Bureau that factored various forms of government aid produced numbers that lowered the poverty threshold. Using government figures from 2002, Besharov and Germanis estimated a family can receive almost $18,000 in noncash benefits a year.

Not every family receives all available benefits. In Long Beach, for instance, the waiting list is 15,000 for Section 8 housing and has been closed.

According to the Weingart Institute for the Study of Homelessness and Poverty, in 1998, only 54 percent of families eligible for food stamps received them.

According to H&R Block, national studies show 25 percent of workers eligible for Earned Income Tax Credits (EITC) do not apply. For families in poverty, EITC can be worth thousands of dollars.

Poor, but with Assets

One set of benchmarks used to dismiss poverty is the amount of goods the poor own.

Robert Rector, Kirk Johnson and Sarah Youssef of the conservative Heritage Foundation think tank wrote in a report that "the count of the 'poor' includes a significant number of relatively well off households who would not be considered impoverished by a common sense definition." The report found high ownership of cars, major appliances and other so-called consumer durables among the poor.

The report also highlighted under-reporting of income and the gap between income and spending. The report says the poor often make money that is not reported, including that from self-employment and the so-called "gray economy," adding that the 1995 Census had the lowest 20 percent making $8,350, but spending $14,607.

The report also said 41 percent of the poor own homes: typically a three bedroom, one-and-a-half bath house in good repair with a carport or garage, porch or patio and a half-acre of land. In Long Beach, that house, without the acreage, would cost about $600,000, according to local Realtor Richard Daskam. A house with that lot size,

Daskam says, would only be found in neighborhoods near Virginia Country Club or Bixby and cost about $1.5 million.

Daskam says those in Long Beach who are poor and own their own homes are typically elderly.

Different Measures Can Be Helpful

On its Web page, the Institute of Research and Poverty has links to nearly 200 groups studying poverty.

Looking at poverty measures, Robert Haveman and Melissa Mullikin of the University of Wisconsin, wrote, "no single poverty measure has a monopoly in identifying the number of people in a nation who are destitute, and the growth and composition of the poor. Each measure contributes to our understanding of the nature of poverty, and hence the consequences and costs of poverty; they are complements, not substitutes."

EVALUATING THE AUTHOR'S ARGUMENTS:

After reading the author's arguments, what factors do you think should be considered when defining poverty? Why?

Poverty in America Is Transitory

Bradley R. Schiller

"The most important picture that emerges from census data is not the size of the poverty population but its transitory nature."

Bradley R. Schiller argues in this viewpoint that poverty is largely transitory for most who experience it. While poverty numbers have remained relatively stable, the composition of those in poverty changes greatly, contends the author. Immigrants and youth, he says, enter and then exit poverty. Poverty, he argues, is rarely a permanent condition. Schiller is a professor of economics at American University and author of *The Economics of Poverty and Discrimination.*

AS YOU READ, CONSIDER THE FOLLOWING QUESTIONS:

1. According to the author, how do poverty rates of immigrants compare with poverty rates of nonimmigrants?
2. Within three years of entering the job market at minimum wage, what percentage of such persons are earning above minimum wage, as stated by Schiller?
3. According to a study cited by the author, what is the "permanent" poverty rate?

The recently released [2006] poverty data paint a grim picture of life in America. Once again the U.S. Census Bureau tells us that 37 million people—one of every 12 residents—is living hand-to-mouth in the United States. This is a shocking statistic, especially in view of our extraordinarily high average incomes (around $60,000 per household), three years of robust economic growth, declining unemployment rates and a dramatic drop in welfare rolls.

Critics of the administration, of course, are quick to interpret this picture. They point to "tax cuts for the rich," punitive welfare reforms, a stagnant federal minimum wage, cutbacks in education and increasingly cutthroat international trade as explanations for both persistent poverty and the widening gap between rich and poor Americans. But whatever merit some of these explanations might have, they are not focused on the right subject. The most important picture that emerges from census data is not the size of the poverty population but its transitory nature.

The Poor Now Are Not the Poor from the Past

The number of people living in poverty has been in a narrow range of 32 million to 37 million for the past 25 years. The 1991 recession briefly pushed the number of poor people up to 39 million; the 1995–99 economic boom shrank it to 31.6 million. The year-to-year changes have been about a million people, up or down.

Although the size of the poverty population has been fairly stable, its composition has not been. The people who were poor in 1981 aren't poor now. The 4 million poor people who were over 65 back then are mostly dead now. The millions of household heads who were unemployed then are probably retired from their jobs. And all those welfare kids being raised by single moms in 1981 are now grown up.

FAST FACT

According to the Heritage Foundation, by 1998, immigrants were three to four times more likely to lack a high school education than were nonimmigrants.

Immigrants and the Young

So who took their place in the poverty ranks? We've got a constant flow of immigrants, for starters. Well over a million immigrants—both legal and illegal—enter the country every year. Most come in at the lowest rungs of the economic ladder, working for the minimum wage or less. The household poverty rates among immigrants are twice as high as those of non-immigrants.

Then we've got 5 million or so low-achieving kids dropping out of high school every year. And more than a million births a year to single moms, about a third of whom are teenagers. On top of that, add more than a million divorces every year that often devastate someone's finances. Then there are the persistent scourges of death, disability and illness—all of which throw families into poverty, often without warning. Finally, there's the economy, in which constantly shifting demands, costs and technology create a continuous profusion of winners and losers. So there's always a flow of new faces into the poverty ranks.

The Transitory Nature of Poverty in America

- Most people remain poor for less than five months.

- Millions of people who fall into poverty due to job loss reenter the labor force and earn enough to rise above poverty.

- For two-thirds of people in poverty, the transition in and out of poverty is relatively quick.

- The number of people who entered and left poverty each year from the mid-1970s through the mid-1990s averaged about 8 million.

- Every five years during the past three decades, between 30 and 40 million Americans have risen out of poverty.

Taken from: *Christian Science Monitor*, May 22, 2006. www.csmonitor.com/2006/0522/p09s02-coop.htm.

Most poor immigrants enter the workforce starting at minimum wage. Within three years of entering the labor market, 85 percent earn more than the federal minimum wage.

Most Escape Poverty Quickly

The outflow is just as impressive. Unemployed workers don't stay unemployed—they do find work and exit the poverty population. Likewise, minimum-wage workers don't keep working for minimum wage. As they gain skills and experience, they command higher wages. Within three years of joining the labor market, 85 percent of minimum-wage entrants (primarily teenagers and immigrants) earn significantly more than the federal minimum.

Immigrants assimilate and move out of poverty as quickly today as in past generations. Most of the single moms will marry (again), gaining the greater economic stability of a two-parent family. Others, perhaps prodded by welfare reforms, will gain employment, particularly once their children start attending school. Inflation-adjusted Social Security and disability benefits will lift millions of older and disabled workers out of poverty.

Poverty Is Rarely Permanent

The reality of our poverty population is constant churn. Some people fall into poverty every year, and just about as many escape its clutches. The popular notion of a "poverty trap" is greatly exaggerated. The flows in and out of poverty are far more impressive than the relatively small subgroup of individuals who stay in poverty for many years. Researchers have observed that three out of five families that fall into poverty in any one year are out of poverty the following year—making poverty a highly transient state.

Even more impressive statistics were collected over a longer period. A University of Michigan study discovered that one out of three U.S. households experienced poverty in at least one year of a 13-year stretch. But only one out of 20 families was poor in at least 10 years, and only one out of 60 stayed poor in all 13 years. Hence, the permanent poverty rate is less than 2 percent, even though the annual poverty rate is closer to 13 percent.

The evident churning in the poverty population doesn't diminish its social importance. But it should change the way we look at poverty statistics and the policy choices we make. We don't have a permanent poverty caste in the United States. Instead we have a very fluid combination of demographic, social and economic forces that propel people in and out of poverty. Policy choices should focus on reducing institutional barriers that slow the poverty outflow and expanding (temporary) safety nets (e.g., unemployment benefits, child support) that reduce the poverty inflow.

EVALUATING THE AUTHOR'S ARGUMENTS:

If the author is correct that poverty is transitory, do you think that means poverty is not a serious problem? Why or why not?

Extreme Poverty Is a Serious Problem Worldwide

"[Extreme] poverty is more pervasive than we thought."

Lesley Wroughton

Lesley Wroughton argues in this viewpoint that extreme poverty is worse than previously thought. The cost of living in developing countries, she says, is higher than previous estimates, resulting in more people living in extreme poverty. While poverty has decreased in some countries, the evidence is compelling, she says, that extreme poverty is likely to increase. Wroughton writes for Reuters news service.

AS YOU READ, CONSIDER THE FOLLOWING QUESTIONS:

1. According to data cited by the author, what percentage of the developing world lives in extreme poverty?
2. What percentage of people in sub-Saharan Africa lives in extreme poverty, according to figures cited by the author?
3. According to a World Bank study cited by the author, what could cause 100 million more people to fall into extreme poverty?

The World Bank said on Tuesday [August 26, 2008] more people are living in extreme poverty in developing countries than previously thought as it adjusted the recognized yardstick for measuring global poverty to $1.25 a day from $1.

The poverty-fighting institution said there were 1.4 billion people—a quarter of the developing world—living in extreme poverty on less than $1.25 a day in 2005 in the world's 10 to 20 poorest countries. Last year, the World Bank said there were 1 billion people living under the previous $1 a day poverty mark.

The new figures are likely to put fresh pressure on big donor countries to move more aggressively to combat global poverty, and on countries to introduce more-effective policies to help lift the poorest.

Even so, the new estimates show how progress has been made in helping the poor over the past 25 years. In 1981, 1.9 billion people were living below the new $1.25 a day poverty line.

Global Price Data Shows Cost of Living Higher

The new estimates are based on updated global price data, and the revision to the poverty line shows the cost of living in the developing world is higher than had been thought. The data is based on 675 household surveys in 116 countries. "These new estimates are a major advance in poverty measurements because they are based on far better price data for assuring that the poverty lines are comparable across countries," said Martin Ravallion, director of the World Bank's Development Research Group.

FAST FACT

Fifty thousand deaths per day occur worldwide as the result of poverty.

While the developing world has more poor people than previously believed, the World Bank's new chief economist, Justin Lin, said the world was still on target to meet a United Nations goal of halving the number of people in poverty by 2015. However, excluding China from overall calculations, the world fails to meet the U.N. poverty targets, Lin said. The World Bank data shows that the number of people living below the $1.25 a day poverty line fell over nearly

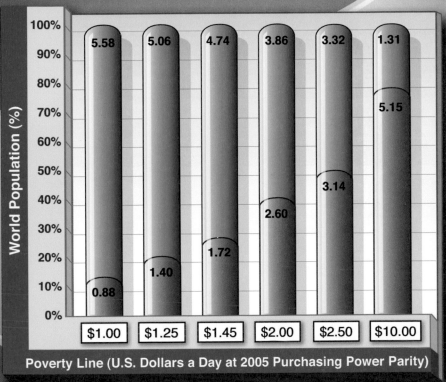

Percent of People in the World at Different Poverty Levels, 2005

Numbers inside bars are world population at that indicator, in billions.

World Population (%)

| 5.58 | 5.06 | 4.74 | 3.86 | 3.32 | 1.31 |

5.15

3.14

2.60

1.72

1.40

0.88

| $1.00 | $1.25 | $1.45 | $2.00 | $2.50 | $10.00 |

Poverty Line (U.S. Dollars a Day at 2005 Purchasing Power Parity)

Taken from: World Bank Development Indicators 2008. www.globalissues.org/article/26/poverty-facts-and-stats.

25 years to 26 percent in 2005 from 52 percent in 1981, a decline on average of about 1 percent a year, he said.

Lin said the new poverty data meant there was no room for complacency and added that rich donor nations need to keep their promises of stepped-up aid to poor countries. "The sobering news that poverty is more pervasive than we thought means we must redouble our efforts, especially in sub-Saharan Africa," said Lin, a leading Chinese academic.

The new figures come ahead of an updated assessment of progress in meeting the U.N.'s Millennium Development Goals, which will be released [September 2007] at a meeting of the U.N. General Assembly.

In sub-Saharan Africa more than 380 million people live below the poverty line.

Regional Variations

While most of the developing world has managed to reduce poverty, the rate in sub-Saharan Africa, the world's poorest region, has not changed in nearly 25 years, according to data using the new $1.25 a day poverty line. Half of the people in sub-Saharan Africa were living below the poverty line in 2005, the same as in 1981. That means about 380 million people lived under the poverty line in 2005, compared with 200 million in 1981.

Elsewhere, poverty has declined.

In East Asia, which includes China, the poverty rate fell to 18 percent in 2005 from almost 80 percent in 1981, when it was the poorest region. In China, the number of people in poverty fell to 207 million from 835 million in 1981.

In South Asia, the poverty rate fell from 60 percent to 40 percent between 1981 and 2005, but that was not enough to bring down the total number of poor in the region, which stood at 600 million in 2005.

In India, the number of people below the $1.25 a day poverty line increased to 455 million in 2005 from 420 million people in 1981. But the share of the population in poverty fell to 42 percent from 60 percent.

The World Bank noted that better-off countries have higher poverty lines and said it was more appropriate in regions such as Latin America and Eastern Europe to use a $2 a day rate.

Poverty Expected to Increase

The bank has estimated that 100 million people could fall into extreme poverty due to soaring food and energy prices. But Ravallion said it will take up to two years before there is clarity on the impact that soaring costs have had on poverty. However, he said early indications from survey data "are pretty convincing that we're going to see increases in poverty as a result of food and fuel prices."

EVALUATING THE AUTHOR'S ARGUMENTS:

Figures cited by the author define "extreme poverty" with reference to the amount of money per day people have to live on. Can you think of factors other than money that could be used to define "extreme poverty"?

Disproportionate Poverty Creates Disadvantages for African Americans in Higher Education

"Black families [are] 3.8 times as likely as white families to be poor."

Theodore Cross and Robert Bruce Slater

The authors of this viewpoint appearing in the *Journal of Blacks in Higher Education* argue that poverty is particularly a problem for African Americans. The income gaps between whites and blacks have changed little over the past forty years, say the authors. Black children are much more likely than whites to grow up in poverty. The authors contend that racial income and wealth inequality make a college education that could lead to higher incomes unattainable for many African Americans. Theodore Cross is the editor and Robert Bruce Slater is the managing editor of *The Journal of Blacks in*

Higher Education, which investigates the status and prospects for African Americans in higher education.

AS YOU READ, CONSIDER THE FOLLOWING QUESTIONS:
1. According to a study cited by the authors, what percentage of black students who dropped out of college did so because of lack of money?
2. The average black family income is what percentage of the average white family's income, according to the authors?
3. What percentage of African American children are living in poverty, according to figures cited by the authors?

The black-white family income and poverty gaps have remained virtually unchanged since the civil rights era of the 1960s. While there are other factors holding blacks back, these very large differences in income and wealth puts a huge drag on the abilities of blacks to make gains in higher education.

The most important barrier to increased black enrollments in higher education is money. Costs of attending state-operated higher educational institutions have sky-rocketed in recent years. Tuition and fees at some private colleges are now close to $50,000 annually. A study by the student loan conglomerate Nellie Mae found that 69 percent of the black students who drop out of college did so because they could not afford the cost of higher education. . . .

FAST FACT

According to a study by the University of Georgia, 26 percent of African Americans in Alabama, Arkansas, Florida, Georgia, Louisiana, Mississippi, North Carolina, South Carolina, Tennessee, Texas, and Virginia are poor.

Racial Income Gap

New data from the U.S. Census Bureau on income and poverty in this country shows the extent of the disadvantages faced by black families, compared to white families, in providing funds for higher education.

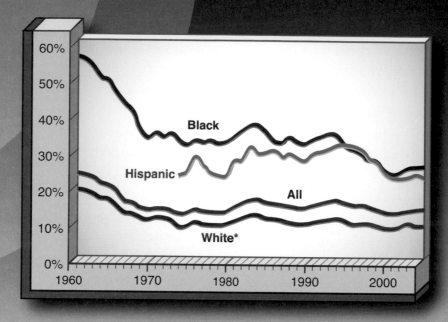

Poverty Rates by Race, 1959–2004

*White is non-Hispanic white from 1973 onward.

Taken from: *Left Business Observer*, 2004. www.leftbusinessobserver.com/IncomePoverty2004.html.

In 2006 white families in the U.S. had a median income of $52,423. For black families, the median income was $31,969. Thus, the average black family in the U.S. had an income that was 61 percent of the income of the average white family. Furthermore, the black-white family income gap has remained virtually unchanged for the past 40 years!

At the high end of the income pyramid, where college costs become more affordable, we find that 21.6 percent of all white families in the United States have incomes of more than $100,000. For blacks, only 9.1 percent of all families have incomes above $100,000.

The difficulty black families face in sending their children to college may also be viewed in new statistics on the nation's poor. The problem is not restricted to the fact that poor families cannot afford to send their children to college. Often these teenagers of college age must enter the work force to help earn money to support their families.

In 2006 there were 9,048,000 African Americans living in poverty. They made up 24.3 percent of the entire black population of the United States. The moderately good news is that there were 120,000 fewer blacks classified as poor in 2006 than was the case in 2005, when 24.9 percent of all African Americans were poor.

The traditional 3 to 1 ratio of blacks to whites in poverty remains unchanged. In 2006 the white poverty rate was 8.2 percent, almost exactly one third the rate for blacks. This 3 to 1 ratio has remained constant throughout the past 40 years.

Black Children Are More Likely to Be Poor

For families, the black-white poverty gap is even wider. In 2006 there were 7,072,000 black families living below the poverty line. They made up 23.1 percent of all black families. For whites, 6.1 percent of all families were classified as poor. Therefore, black families were 3.8 times as likely as white families to be poor.

According to data, the black-white racial income gap has not significantly changed in the last forty years and has contributed to black families being increasingly unable to afford college.

When we look at the figures for children under the age of 18, we find that one third of all African-American children are living in poverty. For whites, 10 percent of all children under 18 are poor.

There are nearly 4 million poor black children in the United States. This group has almost no prospect for obtaining higher education and the success in life that tends to go with the completion of higher education.

Racial Wealth Gap

Family savings and wealth have always been a major source of college tuition payments. Therefore, in measuring the ability to pay for college, we must always take into account the huge racial gap in wealth between blacks and whites in the United States. Wealth in the form of equity in one's home, money in a savings account, or investments in stocks or mutual funds is commonly used to produce income or to act as collateral for a loan to generate funds to pay for higher education.

While the Census Bureau has not released new data on racial differences in family wealth, the latest figures available, which are for the year 2002, show that white families have a median net worth of $88,651. For black families, the median net worth is a mere $5,598.

EVALUATING THE AUTHOR'S ARGUMENTS:

Do the authors explain why African Americans are more likely than whites to be in poverty? Do the statistics cited show that race is the reason, or could there be other explanations?

Chapter 2

What Causes Poverty?

Tent cities for the homeless, such as this one in Reno, Nevada, are starting to appear in many American cities.

The Culture of Poverty Perpetuates Poverty

*"Poverty...
perpetuates
itself...
through a
variety of
self-defeating
habits and
behaviors."*

Cathy Young

Cathy Young argues in this viewpoint that money will not solve the problem of poverty because it is a problem of culture. Multigenerational poverty, she argues, is caused by self-defeating habits and choices. The fact that many immigrant groups started from scratch and achieved the American dream, she says, is proof that poverty is not caused by lack of money. The author contends that changing the culture of poverty is the key to solving the problem of poverty. Young is a contributing editor at *Reason* magazine.

AS YOU READ, CONSIDER THE FOLLOWING QUESTIONS:
1. What examples does the author give of self-defeating habits that cause the culture of poverty?
2. What does Young say would cause most people to have bad cultural habits?
3. What group has the best chance of helping the chronically poor escape the culture of poverty, according to the author?

Cathy Young, "The Problem of Poverty," *The Boston Globe,* October 17, 2005. Reproduced by permission of the author.

After Hurricane Katrina and the devastation left in its wake exposed to the public eye the shocking levels of poverty in the mostly African-American neighborhoods of New Orleans, there was a lot of talk about America's hidden shame and about the need to pay more attention to the plight of the poor when there isn't a natural disaster to put them in the headlines.

Just over a month later, the poor are off the front pages, and the press is far more interested in whether [Supreme Court nominee]

During Hurricane Katrina evacuees waited in line to enter the Superdome in New Orleans. Katrina exposed shocking levels of poverty in the African American communities of the city.

Harriet Miers is a deep legal thinker. Meanwhile, the poor are always with us.

Left and Right Disagree on Poverty

Part of the reason we don't talk much about poverty is that no one really knows what to do about it. Typically, the left [liberals] wants to blame poverty on evil, racist Republicans and to advocate more redistribution of wealth and spending on social programs as the answer. Democratic congressman Charles Rangel of New York recently stated that George W. Bush's inattention to poverty made him our Bull Connor, comparing Bush to the 1960s Alabama police official whose name has become a symbol of racism.

The right [conservatives] meanwhile, tends to blame bloated welfare programs for keeping the poor trapped in their condition, as well as the "culture of poverty" with its deeply entrenched social problems—which, all too often, translates into blaming the poor themselves. After the catastrophe in New Orleans, several conservative websites ran an article by Ayn Rand follower Robert Tracinski, who not only decried

Dropouts Are Broke or in Jail

Dropouts without a GED . . .

- Have an average annual income of $18,734

- Comprise 75 percent of state prison inmates

- Comprise 59 percent of federal inmates

- Are 3.5 times more likely to be incarcerated than high school graduates

- Cost the United States "more than $260 billion . . . in lost wages, lost taxes and lost productivity over their lifetimes."

Taken from: American Youth Policy Forum. www.npr.org/templates/story/story.php?storyid=5300726.

the effects of the welfare state but also referred to New Orleans's poor as "sheep" and "parasites."

Self-Defeating Habits

Most decent people, whatever their politics, will recoil from such dehumanizing rhetoric. But the "culture of poverty" argument itself cannot be so easily dismissed. Yes, some people are poor because of bad luck or catastrophic illness; but chronic, multigenerational poverty is another matter. Yes, poverty in the African-American community results largely from the terrible legacy of a racism that, for generations, denied blacks not only equal opportunity but basic civil rights. But whatever its historical root causes, poverty also perpetuates itself (across racial lines) through a variety of self-defeating habits and behaviors: dropping out of high school, not acquiring marketable job skills, having children without means to support them, even running afoul of the law. In some poor neighborhoods, being a drug dealer is a source of higher status than working in a legitimate job.

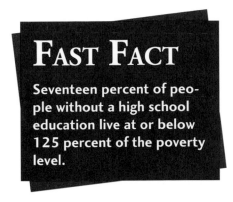

FAST FACT

Seventeen percent of people without a high school education live at or below 125 percent of the poverty level.

Immigrants Have Risen from Poverty

The fact that poverty is a matter of culture, not just money, is illustrated by the immigrant experience. Many immigrants start from scratch when they come to the United States, and succeed in rising out of poverty. For them, the American dream is not a myth. Data from the Urban Institute show that while recent immigrants in 1980 and 1990 were twice as likely as native-born Americans to live in poverty, this disparity disappeared for immigrants who had lived in this country for 10 years or more. (In fact, in 2003, according to the Census Bureau, immigrants who were naturalized US citizens had a slightly higher median income than native-born citizens.) This success story includes black immigrants from the Caribbean and Africa, who on average earn substantially more than native-born African-Americans.

To discuss the culture of poverty is to tread on dangerous ground. One can easily come across as patronizing and condescending, as preaching to the poor from one's middle-class perch—or, worse yet, as bashing the poor for their lack of good character. Here, it's important to remember that good cultural habits are usually not a matter of inherent virtue. Most of us, if born into bad circumstances, would have likely ended up trapped in the same self-defeating patterns.

Changing the Culture of Poverty

Yes, some people manage to overcome multiple social handicaps and break the cultural habits of their environment. But that takes extraordinary energy, determination, and self-sufficiency. Megan McArdle, an editor at *The Economist*, notes on her weblog, Asymmetrical Information, that while conservatives are right in many ways about the causes of poverty, they need to be less moralistic and "a lot more humble."

McArdle also notes that such a diagnosis of the problem leaves us with no ready prescription: Spending more money won't cure poverty, and reforming culture is something that's easier said than done. On the public policy level, we can improve the schools and do something to ease the burden of healthcare costs for men and women in low-paying jobs. But if anyone can change the culture of poverty, it's community activists working in the trenches. And such change is likely to take a long time.

EVALUATING THE AUTHOR'S ARGUMENTS:

Do you believe the author has cited adequate evidence in support of her argument? What additional evidence could make the argument more convincing?

The Culture of Poverty Is a Myth

Paul Gorski

Paul Gorski argues in this viewpoint that the culture of poverty is a myth. The myth, he says, is based upon a collection of stereotypes that are false. The poor, he maintains, are not less hardworking or motivated than are the wealthy. Studies show, he says, that the poor have the same respect for education that the rich have. Poor persons are not, he contends, more likely to use drugs. Gorski is an assistant professor in the Graduate School of Education at Hamline University.

> *"There is no such thing as a culture of poverty."*

AS YOU READ, CONSIDER THE FOLLOWING QUESTIONS:
1. What book does the author say coined the term "culture of poverty," and when was it published?
2. What percentage of children from low-income families have at least one employed parent, according to a study cited by Gorski?
3. According to studies cited by the author, what economic group is more likely to abuse alcohol?

A s the students file out of Janet's classroom, I sit in the back corner, scribbling a few final notes. Defeat in her eyes, Janet drops into a seat next to me with a sigh.

"I *love* these kids," she declares, as if trying to convince me. "I adore them. But my hope is fading."

"Why's that?" I ask, stuffing my notes into a folder.

"They're smart. I know they're smart, but . . ."

And then the deficit floodgates open: "They don't care about school. They're unmotivated. And their parents—I'm lucky if two or three of them show up for conferences. No wonder the kids are unprepared to learn."

At Janet's invitation, I spent dozens of hours in her classroom, meeting her students, observing her teaching, helping her navigate the complexities of an urban midwestern elementary classroom with a growing percentage of students in poverty. I observed powerful moments of teaching and learning, caring and support. And I witnessed moments of internal conflict in Janet, when what she wanted to believe about her students collided with her prejudices.

Like most educators, Janet is determined to create an environment in which each student reaches his or her full potential. And like many of us, despite overflowing with good intentions, Janet has bought into the most common and dangerous myths about poverty.

Chief among these is the "culture of poverty" myth—the idea that poor people share more or less monolithic and predictable beliefs, values, and behaviors. For educators like Janet to be the best teachers they can be for all students, they need to challenge this myth and reach a deeper understanding of class and poverty.

Roots of the Culture of Poverty Concept

[Anthropologist] Oscar Lewis coined the term *culture of poverty* in his 1961 book *The Children of Sanchez*. Lewis based his thesis on his ethnographic studies of small Mexican communities. His studies uncovered approximately 50 attributes shared within these communities: frequent violence, a lack of a sense of history, a neglect of planning for the future, and so on. Despite studying very small communities, Lewis extrapolated his findings to suggest a universal culture of poverty. More than 45 years later, the premise of the culture of poverty

Food Insecurity Affects All Types of Households

Characteristic	1995	1999	2001	2002	2003	2004	2005	2006
All children								
In food-insecure households	19.4	16.9	17.6	18.1	18.2	19.0	16.9	17.2
In households with very low food security among children	1.3	0.7	0.6	0.8	0.6	0.7	0.8	0.6
Poverty status								
Below 100% poverty								
In food-insecure households	44.4	44.0	45.9	45.6	45.2	47.1	42.5	43.6
In households with very low food security among children	3.4	2.2	2.6	2.4	2.0	2.5	2.9	2.1
100–199% poverty								
In food-insecure households	25.4	23.4	27.1	28.4	29.6	28.0	26.4	26.7
In households with very low food security among children	1.4	0.9	0.8	1.2	0.9	1.1	0.8	0.8
200% poverty and above								
In food-insecure households	4.8	5.2	5.5	6.0	6.2	6.2	6.0	6.1
In households with very low food security among children	0.2	0.2	0.1	0.1	0.1	0.1	0.3	0.1
Race								
White, non-Hispanic								
In food-insecure households	14.0	11.0	11.9	12.6	12.0	13.0	12.2	11.8
In households with very low food security among children	0.8	0.4	0.2	0.4	0.2	0.4	0.5	0.3
Black, non-Hispanic								
In food-insecure households	30.6	28.6	29.6	29.4	30.8	31.2	29.2	29.3
In households with very low food security among children	2.3	1.0	1.4	1.3	1.0	1.3	1.9	1.5
Hispanic								
In food-insecure households	33.9	29.3	28.6	29.2	30.8	29.6	23.7	26.0
In households with very low food security among children	2.6	1.3	1.3	1.6	1.6	1.2	1.2	0.7

paradigm remains the same: that people in poverty share a consistent and observable "culture."

Lewis ignited a debate about the nature of poverty that continues today. But just as important—especially in the age of data-driven decision making—he inspired a flood of research. Researchers around the world tested the culture of poverty concept empirically. Others analyzed the overall body of evidence regarding the culture of poverty paradigm.

FAST FACT

About 40 percent of Americans will experience poverty at some point in their lives.

These studies raise a variety of questions and come to a variety of conclusions about poverty. But on this they all agree: *There is no such thing as a culture of poverty.* Differences in values and behaviors among poor people are just as great as those between poor and wealthy people.

In actuality, the culture of poverty concept is constructed from a collection of smaller stereotypes which, however false, seem to have crept into mainstream thinking as unquestioned fact. Let's look at some examples.

The Poor Work as Hard as the Rich

MYTH: Poor people are unmotivated and have weak work ethics.

The Reality: Poor people do not have weaker work ethics or lower levels of motivation than wealthier people. Although poor people are often stereotyped as lazy, [according to the National Center for Children in Poverty] 83 percent of children from low-income families have at least one employed parent; close to 60 percent have at least one parent who works full-time and year-round. In fact, the severe shortage of living-wage jobs means that many poor adults must work two, three, or four jobs. According to the Economic Policy Institute, poor working adults spend more hours working each week than their wealthier counterparts.

The Poor Value Education

MYTH: Poor parents are uninvolved in their children's learning, largely because they do not value education.

The Reality: Low-income parents hold the same attitudes about education that wealthy parents do. Low-income parents are less likely to attend school functions or volunteer in their children's classrooms—not because they care less about education, but because they have less *access* to school involvement than their wealthier peers. They are more likely to work multiple jobs, to work evenings, to have jobs without paid leave, and to be unable to afford child care and public transportation. It might be said more accurately that schools that fail to take these considerations into account do not value the involvement of poor families as much as they value the involvement of other families.

For his 1961 book The Children of Sanchez, *anthropologist Oscar Lewis studied Mexican communities like this one near Mexico City and coined the term "culture of poverty."*

MYTH: Poor people are linguistically deficient.

The Reality: All people, regardless of the languages and language varieties they speak, use a full continuum of language registers. What's more, linguists have known for decades that all language varieties are highly structured with complex grammatical rules. What often are assumed to be *deficient* varieties of English—Appalachian varieties, perhaps, or what some refer to as Black English Vernacular—are no less sophisticated than so-called "standard English."

The Poor Are Not More Likely to Abuse Drugs
MYTH: Poor people tend to abuse drugs and alcohol.

The Reality: Poor people are no more likely than their wealthier counterparts to abuse alcohol or drugs. Although drug sales are more visible in poor neighborhoods, drug use is equally distributed across poor, middle class, and wealthy communities. . . . [In 2003 researchers] found that alcohol consumption is *significantly higher* among upper middle class white high school students than among poor black high school students. Their finding supports a history of research showing that alcohol abuse is far more prevalent among wealthy people than among poor people. In other words, considering alcohol and illicit drugs together, wealthy people are more likely than poor people to be substance abusers.

EVALUATING THE AUTHORS' ARGUMENTS:

After reading this viewpoint and the opposing viewpoint that preceded it, do you believe there is a culture of poverty? Which author best documented her or his point of view?

Economic Colonialism Causes Poverty

Vandana Shiva

"The poor are not those who have been left behind; they are the ones who have been robbed."

Vandana Shiva argues in this viewpoint that economic colonialism has caused much poverty by appropriating the common wealth that sustained societies. Economic colonialism, she says, has created wealth for Europe and North America but created poverty in the counties exploited. Privatizing common wealth for the sake of profit, she argues, has destroyed the economic and social systems that for centuries sustained many societies. Shiva is director of the Research Foundation for Science, Technology, and Natural Resource Policy in New Delhi, India.

AS YOU READ, CONSIDER THE FOLLOWING QUESTIONS:

1. What are the two great economic myths of our times, according to the author?
2. In the author's view, what will be the effect on poverty of further economic development?
3. What is the definition of poor people, as stated by Shiva?

Vandana Shiva, "Two Myths That Keep the World Poor," *CCPA Monitor*, February 1, 2006. Reproduced by permission of Canadian Centre for Policy Alternatives. www.policyalternatives.ca.

From rock singer Bob Geldof to UK politician Gordon Brown, the world suddenly seems to be full of high-profile people with their own plans to end poverty. Jeffrey Sachs, however, is not simply a do-gooder, but one of the world's leading economists, head of the Earth Institute and in charge of a UN panel set up to promote rapid development. So when he launched his book *The End of Poverty*, people everywhere took notice. *Time* magazine even made it into a cover story.

But there is a problem with Sachs's how-to-end poverty prescriptions. He simply doesn't understand where poverty comes from. He seems to view it as the original sin. "A few generations ago, almost everybody was poor," he writes, then adding: "The Industrial Revolution led to new riches, but much of the world was left far behind."

The Poor Have Been Robbed

This is a totally false history of poverty. The poor are not those who have been left behind; they are the ones who have been robbed. The wealth accumulated by Europe and North America is largely based on riches taken from Asia, Africa, and Latin America. Without the destruction of India's rich textile industry, without the takeover of the spice trade, without the genocide of the native American tribes, without African slavery, the Industrial Revolution would not have resulted in new riches for Europe or North America. It was this violent takeover of Third World resources and markets that created wealth in the North and poverty in the South.

Two Economic Myths

Two of the great economic myths of our time allow people to deny this intimate link, and spread misconceptions about what poverty is. First, the destruction of Nature and of people's ability to look after themselves are blamed not on industrial growth and economic colonialism, but on poor people themselves. Poverty, it is stated, causes environmental destruction. The disease is then offered as a cure: further economic growth is supposed to solve the very problems of poverty and ecological decline that it gave rise to in the first place. This is the message at the heart of Sachs's analysis.

The second myth is an assumption that, if you consume what you produce, you do not really produce, at least not economically speaking. If I grow my own food, and do not sell it, then it doesn't contribute to GDP [gross domestic product], and therefore does not contribute towards growth. People are perceived as poor if they eat food they have grown rather than commercially distributed junk foods sold by global agri-business. They are seen as poor if they live in self-built housing made from ecologically well-adapted materials like bamboo and mud rather than in cinder-block or cement houses. They are seen as poor if they wear garments manufactured from handmade natural fibres rather than synthetics.

Sustenance Living Holds Wealth in Common

Yet sustenance living, which the wealthy West perceives as poverty, does not necessarily mean a low quality of life. On the contrary, by their very nature economies based on sustenance ensure a high quality of life when measured in terms of access to good food and water, opportunities for sustainable livelihoods, robust social and cultural identity, and a sense of meaning in people's lives. Because these poor don't share in the perceived benefits of economic growth, however, they are portrayed as those "left behind."

This false distinction between the factors that create affluence and those that create poverty is at the core of Sachs's analysis. And because of this, his prescriptions will aggravate and deepen poverty instead of ending it. Modern concepts of economic development, which Sachs sees as the "cure" for poverty, have been in place for only a tiny portion of human history. For centuries, the principles of sustenance allowed societies all over the planet to survive and even thrive. Limits in Nature were respected in these societies and guided the limits of human consumption. When society's relationship with Nature is

Approximate Timing of Colonialism in Spanish and British Colonies

Spanish Colonies	Onset	Conclusion
Argentina	1580	1819
Bolivia	1538	1825
Chile	1541	1818
Colombia	1536	1819
Costa Rica	1524	1821
Cuba	1511	1899
Dominican Republic	1493	1821
Ecuador	1534	1822
El Salvador	1524	1821
Guatemala	1524	1821
Honduras	1524	1821
Mexico	1521	1821
Nicaragua	1523	1821
Panama	1519	1821
Paraguay	1537	1811
Peru	1533	1824
Uruguay	1625	1828
Venezuela	1528	1821
British Colonies		
Australia	1788	1901
Bahamas	1783	1973
Bangladesh	1756/1857	1947/1971
Barbados	1627	1966
Belize	1798	1981
Botswana	1885	1966
Brunei	1888	1984
Canada	1610/1763	1867
Cyprus	1878	1960

Egypt	**1882**	**1922/1935**
Fiji	**1871**	**1970**
Gambia	**1888**	**1965**
Ghana	**1874**	**1957**
Guyana	**1814**	**1966**
Hong Kong	**1842**	**1999**
India	**1757/1857**	**1947**
Jamaica	**1655**	**1962**
Kenya	**1886**	**1963**
Lesotho	**1884**	**1966**
Malawi	**1891**	**1964**
Malaysia	**1786/1874**	**1957**
Mauritius	**1810**	**1968**
Myanmar	**1826/1885**	**1948**
New Zealand	**1840**	**1907**
Nigeria	**1861/1885**	**1960**
Pakistan	**1857**	**1947**
Sierra Leone	**1787/1896**	**1961**
Singapore	**1819**	**1959**
Solomon Islands	**1893**	**1978**
South Africa	**1795**	**1910**
Sri Lanka	**1798**	**1948**
Sudan	**1898**	**1956**
Swaziland	**1894**	**1968**
Tanzania	**1918**	**1961**
Trinidad/Tobago	**1797**	**1962**
Uganda	**1893**	**1962**
United States	**1607**	**1783**
Zambia	**1890/1923**	**1964**
Zimbabwe	**1895/1923**	**1965/1980**

Taken from: Matthew Lange, James Mahone, and Matthias vom Hau, "Colonialism and Development: A Comparative Analysis of Spanish and British Colonies," *American Journal of Sociology*, 2006.

based on sustenance, Nature exists as a form of common wealth. It is redefined as a "resource" only when profit becomes the organizing principle of society and sets off a financial imperative for the development and destruction of these resources for the market.

Development Destroys Common Wealth

However much we choose to forget or deny it, all people in all societies still depend on Nature. Without clean water, fertile soils, and genetic diversity, human survival is not possible. Today, economic development is destroying these onetime commons, resulting in the creation of a new contradiction: development deprives the very people it professes to help of their traditional land and means of sustenance, forcing them to survive in an increasingly eroded natural world.

A system like the economic growth model we know today creates trillions of dollars of super-profits for corporations while condemning billions of people to poverty. Poverty is not, as Sachs suggests, an initial state of human progress from which to escape. It is a final state people fall into when one-sided development destroys the ecological and social systems that have maintained the life, health and sustenance of people and the planet for ages. The reality is that people do not die for lack of income. They die for lack of access to the wealth of the commons.

Here, too, Sachs is wrong when he says: "In a world of plenty, 1 billion people are so poor their lives are in danger." The indigenous people in the Amazon, the mountain communities in the Himalayas, peasants anywhere whose land has not been appropriated and whose water and biodiversity have not been destroyed by debt-creating industrial agriculture are ecologically rich, even though they earn less than a dollar a day. On the other hand, people are poor if they have to purchase their basic needs at high prices, no matter how much income they make.

Unrestricted Trade Causes Poverty

Take the case of India. Because of cheap food and fibre being dumped by developed nations, and lessened trade protections enacted by the government, farm prices in India are tumbling, which means that the

The author of the viewpoint argues that the book The End of Poverty, *written by Jeffrey Sachs (pictured), and its prescriptions for ending poverty do not work because Sachs does not understand where poverty comes from.*

country's peasants are losing $26 billion (US) each year. Unable to survive under these new economic conditions, many peasants are now poverty-stricken and thousands commit suicide each year. Elsewhere in the world, drinking water is privatized so that corporations can now profit to the tune of $1 trillion a year by selling an essential resource to the poor that was once free. And the $50 billion of "aid" trickling North to South is but a tenth of the $500 billion being sucked in the other direction due to interest payments and other unjust mechanisms in the global economy imposed by the World Bank and the IMF [International Monetary Fund].

If we are serious about ending poverty, we have to be serious about ending the systems that create poverty by robbing the poor of their common wealth, livelihoods, and incomes. Before we can make poverty history, we need to get the history of poverty right. It's not about how much wealthy nations can give, so much as how much less they can take.

EVALUATING THE AUTHOR'S ARGUMENTS:

The author contends that growth and development cause poverty. Are there any positive outcomes from growth and development you can think of that the author failed to consider?

Illegitimacy Causes Poverty

Daily Press

"Young women drop out of school because they're pregnant."

In this viewpoint the *Daily Press* argues that illegitimacy is a cause of poverty. When teens get pregnant, they often drop out of school, says the author. The resulting lack of education, it is contended, makes parents of illegitimate children less able to support themselves and their children. The combination of poverty, low education level, and having a single parent increases the likelihood that children will have health problems, creating another obstacle to escaping from poverty.

AS YOU READ, CONSIDER THE FOLLOWING QUESTIONS:
1. According to the author, how many students become dropouts?
2. By how much has the rate at which women give birth to unplanned children risen, as stated by the author?
3. According to the *Daily Press,* what is the desirable environment for raising children?

T wo news items, coming one after each other, raised the question: is it time to stop playing "Let's pretend"?

As in: Let's pretend that the flood of dropouts doesn't really matter. Let's pretend that the rising tide of illegitimacy doesn't take a toll, on both individuals and society.

Let's pretend that we can, with good intentions and compassion, legislate and appropriate and compensate for the consequences of too many dropouts—at least one in four of our students—and single-parent families—only two-thirds of our children live with both parents. Let's pretend that with enough money and enough programs, we can counteract the effects of poverty.

The author contends that teen pregnancy perpetuates poverty because most pregnant teens drop out of school and are thus less likely to be able to support themselves and their children.

Single-Parent Households

A new study in *Pediatrics*, the journal of the American Academy of Pediatrics, suggests that pretending doesn't stand up to reality. It found that piling social disadvantages on children—the result of poverty, low parental education level and being raised in a single-parent household—has grave health consequences. Children with all three of these "risk factors," as the arid language of academia describes the condition of these children's lives, were four times as likely to have health problems and twice as likely to have chronic problems such as diabetes, asthma or retardation.

FAST FACT

Nearly half of all out-of-wedlock births in New York City are to women who are impoverished.

And here's the part that bursts the bubble of pretense: Having health insurance didn't make any difference.

That means that programs such as Medicaid and FAMIS, Virginia's insurance plan for children in low-income families—which together will consume more than $5 billion in the upcoming state budget—didn't make up for the detrimental effects of parental condition. Taxpayers' contributions, in other words, didn't offset what parents contributed, or weren't able to contribute.

Pregnancy Causes Dropouts

The second bit of news: A study revealed that the rate at which poor women are getting pregnant unintentionally is up 30 percent since the mid-1990s, and the rate at which they are giving birth to unplanned children is up 43 percent. This means a lot more children subject to the ills of poverty.

These problems are inter-related, of course. Young women drop out of school because they're pregnant. They're more likely to drift into pregnancy when they can't see themselves pursuing a path that leads somewhere with real promise, one that requires staying in school. When education goes out the door, poverty comes in, especially when there is just one parent.

Often these parents, whom we would like to see as independent makers of conscious decisions, are really playing out decisions made

Illegitimacy and Teen Births by Race

Out-of-Wedlock Births

Hispanics	45%
Non-Hispanic Whites	24%
Asians	15%
Blacks	68%

Teen Births

Mexican Americans	93 per 1,000 births
Non-Hispanic Whites	27 per 1,000 births
Asians	17 per 1,000 births
Blacks	65 per 1,000 births

For an international comparison, there are 3.9 teen births per 1,000 in Japan and 6.9 per 1,000 in Italy.

Taken from: *City Journal*, 2006. www.city-journal.org/htmal/16_4_hispanic_family_values.html.

by their own parents. Often, they, too, were raised by single mothers, know little about how real fathers function and had scant exposure to alternatives to poverty or to the paths along which education could have taken them.

Parents Who Cannot Support Their Children

This is not to imply, by any means, that programs like Medicaid aren't necessary. The symptoms of poverty must be treated, but that won't solve the problems. All the Head Start and housing vouchers, all the Medicaid and welfare, all the investment in remedial education cannot be counted on to overcome the effect on children of being born to parents who are not prepared to support, nurture and propel them toward a healthy, productive future.

Real progress requires something entirely different. It requires, first, openly acknowledging the underlying problems and frankly assessing their implications, for individuals and communities.

It requires the unrelenting application of pressure on school boards to address the dropout problem, and the mobilization of communities and families to help in what must be a broad-based effort.

It requires collectively reaffirming the truth, from a pragmatic if not a moral point of view, that when men and women have babies whose needs they are not prepared and committed to meet—together, as a functioning family—they are burdening those children and, too often, the community. That there are real consequences to the high rate of out-of-wedlock births to parents who are not in a position to support them.

Two-Parent Families Should Be the Norm

Addressing all this will require individuals, families, communities and all manner of civic organizations to reclaim their stake in the common good and to take stock of the implications of what has evolved in some corners of our society and across the mass culture: a blithe acceptance of unwed parenthood as an acceptable alternative that should not be judged, whose costs should not be counted. These individuals and groups must re-assert their influence on young people, acting swiftly to reclaim those who drift away from school and making clear the expectation that a two-parent family is the desirable environment for raising children.

EVALUATING THE AUTHOR'S ARGUMENTS:

Does the author adequately show the connection between the dropout rate and the illegitimacy rate? What other reasons might account for having a single-parent household?

Poverty May Be a Genetic Problem

Richard Gray

"[The] overactive immune system has developed in poorer communities by being inherited over generations."

Richard Gray argues in this viewpoint that poverty is caused partly by genetics. Research, says the author, shows that a genetic predisposition to overactive immune systems results in accelerated aging and generates chemicals that suppress the natural desire for self-advancement. The tendency to have an overactive immune system, says the author, can be inherited, so generations of poverty tend to self-perpetuate genetically. The immune system's constant state of "alert" stresses the poor, affecting both health and longevity. Gray is a correspondent for *Scotland on Sunday*.

AS YOU READ, CONSIDER THE FOLLOWING QUESTIONS:
1. According to the author, how does an overactive immune system affect the body's supply of spare cells needed to keep aging at bay?
2. What compounds involved in communication within the immune system are much higher in people from deprived areas, according to experts as quoted by Gray?
3. According to the author, what other aspect of well-being relevant to motivation do these compounds affect?

Scottish scientists have discovered a "poverty gene" which causes people from deprived areas to age rapidly, pass on health problems to the next generation and might even explain negative attitudes to employment.

Research in Glasgow has established that deprivation can lead to an overactive immune system which quickly uses up the body's supply of spare cells needed to keep ageing at bay. It means a typical 55-year-old from the city's East End might have a "biological age" closer to 70.

Centuries of natural selection among poor communities mean those with highly active immune systems are more likely to pass their genes on, condemning the next generation to grow old before their time. Most astonishing of all, it is suspected that a hyperactive immune system floods the brain with a cocktail of chemicals which suppress the natural desire for self-advancement.

Genetics and Poverty Are Linked

The study, by the Glasgow Centre for Population Health, is the first time the full extent of the link between health, genetics and poverty has been looked at scientifically. The findings have been seized upon by health campaigners as evidence that poverty is not simply the result of idleness and that more resources should be ploughed into tackling health inequality to break the cycle of deprivation.

> **FAST FACT**
>
> A 2004 study of genetic and environmental differences among 1,116 mothers and their five-year-old same-sex twins found that genes explained 70 percent of the variability in children's behavioral resilience and 46 percent of the difference in their cognitive ability.

But fears have also been expressed that linking poverty to genetic traits could have the opposite effect by encouraging the view that the poor should be abandoned as a lost cause.

Scotland has one of the worst health records in the western world, with shockingly high levels of chronic illnesses such as heart disease, obesity, cancer and diabetes.

There are enormous health gaps within Scotland, with men living in Glasgow's East End expected to die by the age of 64 while in Orkney life expectancy is 82.

Initial findings from the new research have shown that those from poorer areas are hit with a 'double whammy' of unhealthy environmental factors and an inherited predisposition to poor health.

Overactive Immune Systems

Dr Chris Packard, a biochemist and principal investigator in the study, said:

> We are looking at the idea that these people suffer from a chronic state of inflammation where their immune systems are constantly on a high state of alert.
>
> Compounds called cytokines, which talk to other parts of the immune system to prepare it for the invasion of bacteria, are far higher in people from deprived areas compared with the more affluent ones.
>
> This constant state of alert seems to be prematurely ageing the body beyond chronological age and so accelerates chronic diseases—they are, in a sense, old beyond their years.

Packard believes this overactive immune system has developed in poorer communities by being inherited over generations. He claims that children with more aggressive biological defences were better able to survive potentially deadly Victorian-era diseases such as measles and so were able to pass on this trait to their own children.

This has led to large swathes of deprived communities who have lived for generations in the same area, now suffering from high levels of immune activity. While this can provide protection during childhood against diseases, it causes additional stress to the body in adulthood, which causes it to age far faster.

Using Up Spare DNA

This ageing process can be gauged by measuring the growing thickness of artery walls. The team are also studying the spare DNA that helps cells to replicate to repair tissue damaged by wear and tear. With

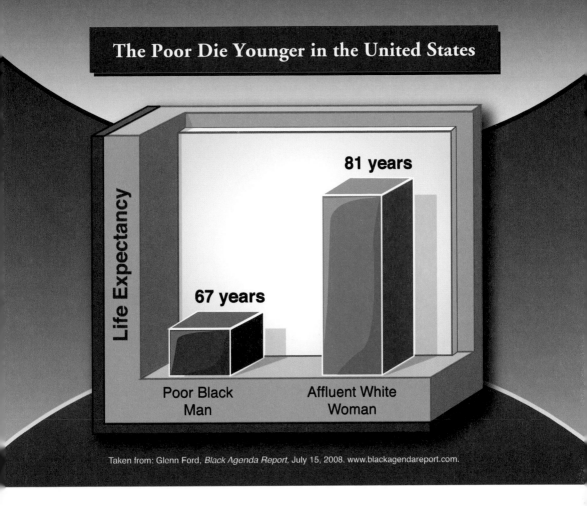

Life Expectancy

81 years

67 years

Poor Black
Man

Affluent White
Woman

Taken from: Glenn Ford, *Black Agenda Report*, July 15, 2008. www.blackagendareport.com.

each replication this DNA reduces, and once it is gone the cells can no longer replicate, meaning tissues degenerate.

Packard said: "If you look at a person from the East End of Glasgow aged 55, they may look closer to 65 or 70, while those from a more affluent area of the same age will probably be far closer to their real age."

The researchers are also conducting brain scans on individuals in a bid to unravel the effect this high-level immunity has on their psychology.

Cytokines Create Negative Attitudes

Packard added: "Cytokines also affect mood and an individual's general mental outlook to make them feel very negative about their life. This may explain why people from these deprived

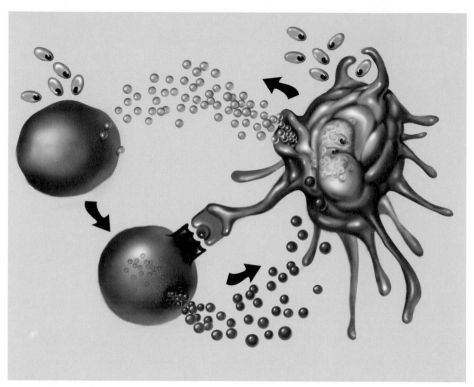

Pictured is an illustration of how white blood cells arm themselves against parasites. White blood cells release cytokine interleukin 1, which helps activate helper T cells. The T cells in turn release the cytokine interferon gamma, which enhances the white cells' ability to engulf and destroy the invading microorganisms.

backgrounds feel they are trapped in poverty and are unable to see the benefits of changing their lifestyle to improve their health. They feel very negatively about life and cannot see the point in trying to extend it."

The researchers now hope to find new ways of helping people from deprived areas to improve their health. Shona Robison, SNP [Scottish National Party] shadow health minister, said it was important the government made it easier for poorer people to pull themselves out of poverty. "My concern is that we don't start pushing responsibility for dealing with poverty and poor health on to individuals themselves," she said. "We can't write off whole generations of families as being damaged by poverty, as given support through improved economic conditions and education, they can turn their lives around."

Not Everyone Agrees

But Lord Tebbit, the former Trade and Industry Secretary who famously urged the unemployed to "get on their bikes", said he did not believe poverty could be explained by genetics.

He said:

> My sorrow is that on the left of politics these days, there is a great deal of running away from the sort of politics of the left in the Welsh valleys during the late 19th and early 20th century, where they didn't feel they had to be bound by poverty and fought their way out of it, partly through very high standards of education. The incentive to be a success is far higher in poor areas, which is why you frequently get individuals springing up to do very well from deprived backgrounds.

Professor Allyson Pollock, an expert on health inequalities at the Centre for International Public Health Policy, warned that linking poverty to genetics could lead to the idea that the poor were somehow inferior. "Poverty is not a genetic issue, it is an economic issue. If you go down that route you may end up with eugenics, and that is extremely worrying," she said.

EVALUATING THE AUTHOR'S ARGUMENTS:

If poverty is caused by genetics, does this mean that programs to reduce poverty are pointless? Why or why not?

Chapter 3

How Can Poverty Be Reduced?

Habitat for Humanity's work project in Mississippi refurbishes old houses in just one of the private sector's volunteer programs to fight poverty.

Government Programs Reduce Poverty

Arloc Sherman

"The U.S. system of public benefits ... reduces both the extent and depth of poverty while ensuring that millions of Americans have access to medical care."

Arloc Sherman argues in this viewpoint that public benefits lift a significant number of people out of poverty and reduce the poverty of those who remain poor. In addition, says the author, for many people government-provided health insurance is the only health insurance they have. Public benefits, he contends, are especially important to the elderly and for families with children. Sherman is an analyst for the Center on Budget and Policy Priorities.

AS YOU READ, CONSIDER THE FOLLOWING QUESTIONS:

1. According to the author, by how much do public benefits reduce the number of Americans living in poverty?
2. For how many Americans is government-program health insurance their only source of health insurance, as stated by Sherman?
3. According to the author, by what percentage did public benefits reduce the number of elderly living in poverty?

Arloc Sherman, "Public Benefits: Easing Poverty and Ensuring Medical Coverage," Center on Budget and Policy Priorities, August 17, 2005. Reproduced by permission.

When individuals and families experience crises such as job loss, illness, disability, or divorce, they may face the prospect of falling into poverty (or becoming poorer) and losing health insurance coverage. Various government assistance programs are designed to lessen these hardships. These programs also provide support when families work but have low earnings and when people reach retirement age.

Effects on Poverty and Health

An examination of Census data shows that as a whole, the U.S. public benefits system, sometimes referred to as the "safety net," has the following effects on poverty and health insurance status.

- It cuts the number of Americans living in poverty almost in half. . . .
- It reduces the severity of poverty for those who remain poor. Without these programs, these families would have average disposable income equal to 29 percent of the poverty line. With the programs, their average income rises to 57 percent of the poverty line.
- It provides health care coverage to tens of millions of individuals who otherwise would be uninsured.

Two Types of Programs

There are two principal categories of public benefit programs—those that provide benefits regardless of income and those that limit assistance to people with low or modest incomes. The first category of programs includes the major social insurance programs such as Social Security, unemployment insurance, and Medicare. Programs in the second category are often referred to as "means-tested" programs [programs that are restricted to families or individuals with incomes below a particular level].

Means-tested programs play a large role in reducing the extent and severity of poverty and providing health care to low-income Americans. Some 11 million low-income Americans are lifted above the poverty line by means-tested benefits, and more than 55 million receive health insurance from the means-tested medical programs, Medicaid and SCHIP [State Children's Health Insurance Program]. Most of these people would otherwise be uninsured.

This analysis provides an overview of the role of income support programs in reducing poverty and the role of health insurance programs in providing access to needed health care. It also examines the effects of these programs on different demographic groups and how the effects of these programs compare with the effects of comparable programs in other countries. The programs examined here could be strengthened, as is indicated by the continuing existence of significant poverty in the United States and the large number of individuals who lack health insurance as well as by the fact that other wealthy industrialized nations provide stronger assistance (particularly for low-income families with children) and generally have lower poverty rates. Nevertheless, the strengths of the public benefits programs in the United States are impressive.

Public Income Support Cuts Poverty Nearly in Half

Public income support in the United States comes from programs that are not limited to people with low incomes, such as Social Security and unemployment insurance, and from means-tested programs, which are targeted by income. The means-tested programs include traditional income assistance, such as that provided by the Temporary Assistance for Needy Families (TANF) and Supplemental Security Income (SSI) programs, and "near-cash" benefits, such as food assistance and housing subsidies, which are not provided in cash but are used to pay regular monthly bills. Certain tax credits, such as the Earned Income Tax Credit (EITC), are also means-tested.

To examine the combined effect of these programs, we analyzed Census Bureau data on families' disposable income—that is, their incomes after subtracting income and payroll taxes and adding all cash income assistance, food assistance, housing subsidies, and energy assistance benefits. This analysis accounts for . . . public benefits including cash payments, tax credits, and near-cash assistance. An analysis of Census data for 2003 (the latest year for which these data are available) shows that:

- Public income-support programs lifted 27 million Americans above the poverty line. That is, the programs reduced the number of Americans with disposable income below the poverty line from 58 million people when income from the programs is not considered to slightly less than 31 million when it is counted. This constitutes a reduction of 47 percent in the number of people who lived in poverty.

- Among those who remained in poverty, these programs eased the severity of poverty by lifting the average poor person from 29 percent of the poverty line when this assistance is not considered to 57 percent of the poverty line with this assistance.
- Means-tested benefits and tax credits alone lifted nearly 11 million Americans above the poverty line. Stated differently, in the absence of the income that these means-tested policies provide, more than 41 million Americans would have had income below the poverty line in 2003. Counting the means-tested benefits and tax credits, the number in poverty was reduced to just under 31 million.
- Means-tested policies play a particularly important role in reducing the *severity* of poverty among those whose incomes remain below the poverty line. On average, poor people have family income that equals just 39 percent of the poverty line when all income is counted *except* income from means-tested benefits and refundable tax credits. When means-tested benefits and tax credits are counted, the average disposable income of poor individuals rises to 57 percent of the poverty line.

When Public Health Insurance Is the Only Health Insurance

U.S. programs and policies provide health insurance coverage for eligible elderly people, low-income families with children, and individuals with severe disabilities. The two principal public health insurance programs are Medicare, for seniors and many non-elderly individuals with disabilities, and Medicaid, for low-income children, families, the elderly, and individuals with disabilities. Closely related to Medicaid is the State Children's Health Insurance Program (SCHIP), which provides health insurance to children whose families earn too much to qualify for traditional Medicaid but nevertheless have low incomes. All together, the programs provide health insurance for over 80 million Americans each month, administrative records show. The means-tested medical programs, Medicaid and SCHIP, provide coverage for more than 55 million low-income people over the course of a year, including some low-income individuals for whom Medicaid pays their Medicare premiums and deductibles.

The combination of Social Security, Supplemental Security Income (SSI), food stamps, Medicare, and Medicaid government programs for the elderly has reduced the overall number of seniors living in poverty.

The majority of Medicaid enrollees lack any other health insurance during the year. Census data for 2003 show that:

- Four of five people enrolled in *Medicaid* or *SCHIP* had no private insurance during the year and relied exclusively on public health coverage.
- Two of five Medicare enrollees had no private insurance during the year and relied exclusively on public health care coverage.

- More than 40 million Americans received their only health insurance during the year from government programs.
- Another 45 million Americans had no health insurance at all.

It is worth noting that federal policies affect the health insurance status of more Americans than those covered by Medicare, Medicaid, and SCHIP. Many Americans are affected by federal tax exclusions and deductions for health insurance, and the federal government directly insures millions of federal employees, military personnel, and their dependents, and provides health care to veterans. This analysis focuses on the main public health insurance programs—Medicare Medicaid, and SCHIP.

Anti-Poverty Efforts Help Some Groups More than Others

The effectiveness of U.S. anti-poverty policies varies by age and other factors. Public benefit programs are most effective at reducing poverty among the elderly. Although these programs are considerably less effective at reducing poverty among families with children, they still lift 4.6 million otherwise-poor children above the poverty line.

The U.S. system of public benefits is weakest for poor adults who are not elderly or disabled and not raising minor children. These individuals seldom are eligible for either income assistance or health care coverage. The safety net also is much weaker for legal immigrants, many of whom now are barred because of their immigrant status from programs for which they otherwise would qualify.

Effectiveness for the Elderly

The nation's most potent income-security policies are for the elderly. The combination of Social Security, SSI, food stamps, and other programs reduced the overall number of seniors living in poverty in 2003 by 14 million (more than 80 percent), and lifted the disposable income of those remaining in poverty from an average of just 8 percent of the poverty line to 62 percent of the poverty line. In addition, Medicare and Medicaid combine to provide health insurance for virtually all of the 35 million Americans age 65 and older.

Even for seniors, gaps in the safety net remain. In many cases, Social Security payments are not large enough to lift recipients out of poverty, and some retirees (such as domestic or seasonal workers whose past employers failed to pay the required Social Security payroll taxes) may receive little or no Social Security benefit. Seniors who qualify for small or no Social Security benefits are supposed to be covered by the Supplemental Security Income program, but SSI pays a maximum federal benefit that is 27 percent below the poverty line for an individual living alone. Partly as a result, 3.1 million seniors had disposable family incomes below the poverty line in 2003, even after all benefits are counted.

Another 13.7 million seniors remained barely above this income range, with disposable incomes between one and two times the poverty line (between $8,825 and $17,650 a year in 2003 for a senior living alone). While seniors are the *least* likely age group to live below the poverty line, they are the *most* likely age group to be *just above* the poverty line. (It should be noted that many near-poor seniors are not counted as poor because of a quirk in the poverty line itself. The federal poverty line is set 8 to 10 percent lower for elderly single individuals and couples than for similar non-elderly individuals and couples. Most of the elderly live alone or with a spouse. If the poverty definition were adjusted to use the same poverty line for the elderly as for the non-elderly, the poverty rate for seniors would be slightly higher, rather than lower, than the poverty rate for younger adults.)

FAST FACT

Medicaid covers more than 50 million of the poorest Americans, including the elderly, the disabled, and children and their mothers.

Effectiveness for Families with Children

Public benefits also substantially reduce the amount and severity of poverty for families with children, although not nearly to the same degree as they do for seniors. Government benefits lifted nearly one of every three otherwise-poor children above the poverty line in 2003. For millions of other poor children, poverty was made less severe than it otherwise would have been.

Over the past two decades, the nature of the safety net has changed markedly for families with children. Assistance has expanded for low-income working families with children; low-income working families

Public Benefits Reduce Poverty by Nearly Half

The following illustrates the number of Americans below the poverty line before and after counting public benefits and taxes in 2003.

Poverty status is based on family disposable income (after taxes and counting near-cash benefits).

Taken from: CEPP tabulations of March 2004 Current Population Survey.

can now receive a stronger federal earned income tax credit (EITC), greater federal and state child care assistance, and greater health insurance coverage, among other supports. Most families with children that are lifted above the poverty line by public benefits are working families.

At the same time, protections have weakened for the poorest families (those with very low or no earnings) due to restrictions in TANF [Temporary Assistance for Needy Families] income assistance. To be eligible for income assistance through TANF, families typically must have incomes far below the poverty line. Despite this, the federal government estimates that only about half of families with children that are poor enough to qualify for TANF income assistance now receive it. In the mid-1990s, about 80 percent of families who qualified for the predecessor AFDC [Aid to Families with Dependent Children] program received income assistance.

Many poor families also are being left deeper in poverty due in part to the overall reduction in the amount of income assistance provided through the TANF program. A poor child now is more likely to experience deep poverty than was the case a decade ago. Nearly one in three poor children (31 percent) had disposable income below *half* of the poverty line in 2003, compared with fewer than one in four (23 percent) in 1995.

Immigrants and Non-Elderly Childless Individuals

The U.S. safety net is weakest for two other groups—immigrants and non-elderly individuals without children. For immigrant families, eligibility for safety-net programs ranging from food stamps to medical assistance was sharply restricted in the mid-1990s. These cuts have been restored only partially in the years since then. In 2002, low-income people in families headed by an immigrant were only half as likely as Americans overall to have their family income lifted above the poverty line by public benefits.

For individuals who are not raising minor children (and are not elderly or disabled), cash income support and publicly-funded health insurance are not widely available, and housing programs give low priority to serving such people. Even the food stamp program, which has relatively few limitations on eligibility for those who meet its financial requirements, imposes much more severe restrictions on these individuals. Most individuals between the ages of 18 and 50 who do not have disabilities and are not raising minor children are eligible for food stamps for only three months while out of work in any 36-month period. The safety net largely bypasses these individuals, doing little to lessen the severity of their poverty. In addition, federal and state tax policies actually tax this group somewhat deeper into poverty.

Public Benefits Are Stronger, More Effective in Other Countries

Public benefit programs in the United States could be stronger. This can be seen by a comparison with other nations. Most other Western industrialized nations have more effective anti-poverty policies—and lower poverty rates—than does the United States, especially for children.

Research by economist Timothy M. Smeeding, one of the foremost experts on public benefit programs in developed nations, has shown that government cash and non-cash benefits and tax credits in the United State lift only 1 in 9 otherwise-low-income children to half of the national median income. The equivalent programs in Canada lift 1 in 3 such children to half of that country's median income. In Britain, Germany, the Netherlands, Belgium, and other countries, the figure is more than 1 in 2.

Smeeding also found that children at the bottom of the economic ladder in the United States tend to have lower real incomes, with less buying power, than their counterparts in these other nations. Thus, the poorest 25 percent of American children have lower family incomes than do the poorest 25 percent of Canadian children. And the poorest 22 percent of American children have lower income than the poorest 22 percent of German children. This is the case even though the United States is a wealthier nation overall, with a higher per-capita gross domestic product.

The United Kingdom provides an example of how a nation can make significant strides against poverty. The British government stepped up its anti-poverty efforts markedly after Prime Minister Tony Blair pledged in 1999 to end child poverty within 20 years and cut it in half in ten years. To achieve this ambitious poverty reduction goal, the United Kingdom has strengthened public benefits and provided new work supports such as child care and a U.S.-style EITC to families. Smeeding calculates that the proportion of British children who would be considered below the poverty line by U.S. standards has dropped since 1999 by more than one-third.

Benefits Lift People Out of Poverty

The U.S. system of public benefits achieves important objectives. It reduces both the extent and depth of poverty while ensuring that millions of Americans have access to medical care. This system lifts 27 million people out of poverty and provides health insurance to tens of millions of people who otherwise would be uninsured.

Both social insurance programs and programs targeted on low-income Americans play an important role. Social Security lifts millions of seniors and families in which a breadwinner has become disabled or has died out of poverty. Programs such as the EITC, SSI, and food stamps help those who receive little or no help from the social insurance programs to meet basic needs. The means-tested assistance programs lift 11 million Americans out of poverty.

In addition, public health insurance programs—Medicare, Medicaid, and SCHIP—provide access to medical care to more than one in four Americans including nearly all of the nation's elderly. Without these programs, the ranks of the uninsured—already 45 million strong—would be far more numerous.

EVALUATING THE AUTHOR'S ARGUMENTS:

Does the author contend that public benefits reduce poverty or that public benefits lessen the effect of poverty? Is there a difference between these two ideas? Explain why or why not.

Government Programs Do Not Reduce Poverty

Matthew Ladner

"The causes of poverty have proven to be complex, and the ability of government to affect them has been limited."

Matthew Ladner argues in this viewpoint that government programs do not reduce poverty. Analyzing data on a state-by-state basis, the author contends that states that spend more on government programs showed increases in poverty while those who spent less showed decreases. Lower government spending results in low taxes, he argues, which in turn promotes economic growth that benefits the poor much more than government poverty programs. Ladner is vice president for policy research at the Goldwater Institute.

AS YOU READ, CONSIDER THE FOLLOWING QUESTIONS:

1. According to the author, when, in relation to the War on Poverty, did most of the decline in American poverty occur?
2. By how much did poverty rates increase in the top-ten spending states, according to figures cited by Ladner?
3. According to the author, how did state spending correlate with childhood poverty?

Matthew Ladner, "How to Win the War on Poverty: An Analysis of State Poverty Trends," Goldwater Institute Policy Report, November 14, 2006. Reproduced by permission.

W hat role should the government play in reducing poverty? For centuries, that question had a rather straightforward answer: not much. In medieval Europe, for example, conventional thinking understood poverty as the product of character flaws, such as indolence or drunkenness. Government left the function of reducing poverty to religious and private charitable organizations.

Antipoverty History

The first antipoverty legislation, Britain's Poor Laws of 1601, very much reflected this traditional thinking. The law distinguished between the "worthy" and "non-worthy" poor. The law defined the "worthy poor" as those unable to work through no fault of their own—those having suffered a debilitating injury or a widowed mother with children, for example. The "non-worthy poor" included everyone else, and certainly everyone who was able-bodied. The law kept the amount of aid strictly minimal, well below what a person could earn by working.

In the United States, a similar philosophy lasted until the advent of the Great Depression in 1929, when the nation experienced a prolonged economic crisis, with mass unemployment. Politicians of the time blamed the downturn on "big business" and the "plutocrats" of the roaring 1920s.

President Franklin D. Roosevelt responded to the crisis by vastly increasing the size and scope of government in the area of poverty reduction. Economic historians now understand that the Federal Reserve and the [Herbert] Hoover and Roosevelt administrations exacerbated and prolonged the downturn with a series of policy mistakes. Monetary, trade, and labor market policy blunders worsened the Great Depression.

Politically, however, Roosevelt's administration received credit for fighting the Depression. Roosevelt created the political and intellectual foundation for governmental antipoverty efforts at the federal and subsequently the state levels.

These efforts reached their crescendo with President [Lyndon] Johnson's War on Poverty programs, the apex of the American government's antipoverty efforts. Johnson transformed government ambitions from simply alleviating poverty to actually eliminating poverty. Within a decade, a powerful backlash against such programs began.

President [Ronald] Reagan famously quipped that "Some years ago the United States declared war on poverty, and poverty won." Reagan's jest reflected a concern that government antipoverty programs not only had failed to reduce poverty but actually contributed to an increase in poverty. [Author] Charles Murray's critique of the welfare system's perverse incentives discouraging work and marriage, for example, eventually led to major welfare reform in 1996. Despite dire warnings of catastrophe from some, welfare reforms achieved substantial reductions in poverty rates.

Despite recent changes in welfare policy, many of the War on Poverty programs continue to this day. Some, such as Medicaid, remain major drivers of state budgets.

Competing Models for Poverty Reduction

In broad terms, there are two strategies for poverty reduction: state government growth and private-sector growth. . . .

According to classical liberal thought, government should keep taxes and spending at the lowest possible levels. Governments should also avoid burdensome and counterproductive regulation of the private economy. Classical liberals argue that this model produces superior rates of economic growth, which in turn lead to a sustained reduction in poverty. George Mason University economist Tyler Cowen, for example, notes that had the United States grown one percentage point less per year between 1870 and 1990, the America of 1990 would be no richer than the Mexico of 1990. Cowen also notes the compound power of economic growth by calculating that at an annual growth rate of 5 percent, it takes just over 80 years for a country to move from a per capita income of $500 to a per capita income of $25,000 in constant dollars. At a growth rate of 1 percent, such an improvement takes 393 years.

The influence of economic growth on poverty rates can be seen in examining data from the post–World War II period. . . .

The majority of the decline in poverty occurred before the advent of War on Poverty programs of the mid-1960s. The postwar economic boom, which roared through the 1950s and into the early

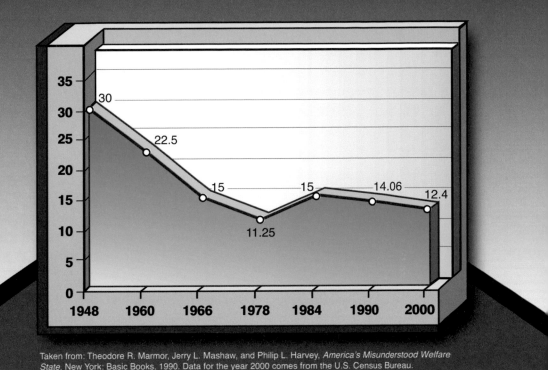

United States Poverty Rate, 1948–2000

Taken from: Theodore R. Marmor, Jerry L. Mashaw, and Philip L. Harvey, *America's Misunderstood Welfare State.* New York: Basic Books, 1990. Data for the year 2000 comes from the U.S. Census Bureau.

1970s, ultimately served as the catalyst for a dramatic decline in the poverty rate. Likewise, the economic difficulties of the late 1970s and early 1980s increased the poverty rate. The national poverty rate has been stuck in double-digits since the mid-1960s.

At the national level, the progress of the postwar boom eventually faded. . . .

Does State Spending Reduce Poverty?

Fighting poverty is a major justification for state spending. However, does state government spending actually reduce poverty? Big-spending governments did a poor job of reducing poverty during the 1990–2000 period. . . .

Although there are doubtlessly some who benefit from high state government spending, the poor do not seem to be among them. The 10 states with the lowest per capita spending enjoyed a sizable reduction in overall poverty rates, approaching twice the national average. However, the top 10 big spenders not only failed to reduce poverty rates, but they actually suffered an *increase* in poverty rates of 7.3 percent.

Often, advocates justify high government spending on behalf of children. . . .

It is hard to imagine anyone disagreeing with the goal of promoting the well-being of children and families. The advocated means to achieving the goal, however, seem quite suspect. . . .

FAST FACT

Medicaid expenditures constitute 22 percent of state government budgets.

Low-spending states experienced substantial declines in childhood poverty rates. Meanwhile, the highest spending states suffered an actual *increase* in childhood poverty. During this period, the average state saw childhood poverty decline by 8.4 percent, but in the 10 highest-spending states, childhood poverty increased by 4.5 percent. Meanwhile, the average reduction in childhood poverty in the states with the lowest state and local spending per capita was 45 percent greater than the average state's spending.

Taxes Harm Poor

Does it follow then that state government spending directly causes poverty? Not necessarily. Government spending ultimately derives from taxes. The American federal system presents a variety of choices for individuals and businesses in terms of where they wish to live and do business. States with relatively high tax rates suffer greatly from the process of emigration—that is, people and businesses leave high-tax states for low-tax states. Such movements respectively damage and reward state economies according to their fiscal and regulatory choices. Apparently, high taxes inflict more harm than spending does good for the poor.

Tax Rates and Poverty

The data show that big-spending states were very ineffective at reducing poverty rates. If classical liberals are correct that lower

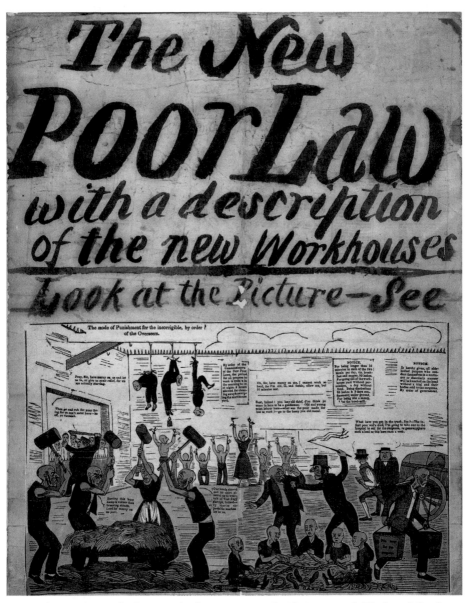

Britain's Poor Laws of 1601 was the first antipoverty legislation passed. The law defined "worthy poor" as those unable to work through no fault of their own and "unworthy poor," which included everyone else.

taxes will result in higher economic growth and thus in lower rates of poverty, we should be able to find evidence of this in state economic statistics. . . .

[According to U.S. Census Bureau data from 1990 and 2000] low-tax states saw a decline in poverty rates more than twice as large as the average state decline (–13.7 percent decline compared with –6 percent). Poverty rates increased in the high-tax states by 3 percent.

Again, the same pattern holds [for childhood poverty rate trends for the same states]. The high tax states badly underperform when compared with the average and do much worse in comparison to the low-tax states.

Again, low-tax states substantially outperformed both the national average and the high-tax states in reducing poverty. In fact, the low-tax states experienced a reduction in childhood poverty more than four times larger than the high-tax states.

The dramatic declines in poverty in the "small government" states strongly confirm the classical liberal hypothesis: Low spending and low taxes promote economic growth, which in turn reduces poverty. These states seem to have succeeded in reducing poverty by allowing the private economy to flourish. . . .

In the fight against poverty, it is clear that less is more. We cannot know all the reasons high-tax and -spending states proved so inept at reducing poverty during the 1990s. Some broad explanations, however, should be considered.

Growth Reduces Poverty

First, the failure of many government programs to reduce poverty should instill policymakers with a sense of humility. The causes of poverty have proven to be complex, and the ability of government programs to affect them has been limited.

Second, despite the apparent complexity poverty poses to government agencies, economic growth has proven to be an effective tonic in reducing poverty. Private-sector growth possesses much greater power in the fight against poverty than do government programs. Government spending beyond what is necessary to ensure law, order, and property rights provides limited economic returns. Although advocates justify high taxes for the sake of the poor and children, the truth of the matter is that taking money out of the private sector slows job creation and income growth. The economy then creates fewer private-sector employment opportunities, meaning there will be less competition for labor, both skilled and unskilled. Ultimately, those looking for the first rung on the economic ladder will be the most vulnerable victims of this process. The best antipoverty program is a four-letter word: jobs. Taxes and regulation destroy them.

The Wealthy Gain from Government Spending

Second, the Robin Hood mythology of state as antipoverty crusader requires serious reexamination. Economists term the pursuit of government subsidy, whether through direct government appropriation or through the tax code, as "rent seeking." Rent seeking represents an alternative way to seek riches. Justifying a subsidy to a handful of politicians, rather than producing something for which people will voluntarily hand over their money, can grant enormous fortunes.

Accordingly, we should not be surprised that the poor suffered in high-spending states. Wealthy interests possess enormous advantages over the poor in the process of rent seeking. The poor vote, participate in civic organizations, make campaign contributions, and hire lobbyists at very low rates. The wealthy pursue all these activities at much higher rates. Progressives implicitly assume that government spending will help the poor as if a nonpolitical board of altruists set fiscal policy.

The reality is quite different. Politicians set fiscal policy in an entirely political context. Rather than a Federal Reserve peopled by figurative Mother Teresas, politicians in competitive democratic races make decisions about state taxing and spending. High-tax and -spending states dole out a great deal of "rent," but we should not be shocked to find that it is the powerful, rather than the powerless, who benefit. Outside of fairytales, Robin Hood often takes from the poor and gives to the rich.

EVALUATING THE AUTHOR'S ARGUMENTS:

The author correlates government spending with poverty and argues that one causes the other. Can you think of reasons why states experiencing poverty might need to spend more than states with less poverty?

Conditional Cash Transfers Contribute to Reduced Poverty

"Cash transfers, with strings attached, are a better way of helping the poor."

The Economist

In this viewpoint the author argues that conditional cash transfers (CCTs) can help reduce poverty. The author contends that CCTs tie conditions to poverty assistance that encourage behaviors that will prevent future poverty, such as vaccinations and staying in school. CCTs are being tried throughout Latin America, and evaluations, says the author, show that they are effective. The following viewpoint is excerpted from an article appearing in *The Economist,* a magazine covering business and political news.

AS YOU READ, CONSIDER THE FOLLOWING QUESTIONS:
1. According to the author, under Mexico's program, what happens to cash payments if a child in the family misses more than 15 percent of class days?
2. How does the cost of Brazil's CCT program compare to the cost of social insurance schemes, according to the author?
3. How did CCTs affect dropout rates in Mexico, according to *The Economist?*

C ash transfers, with strings attached, are a better way of helping the poor than many previous social programmes, as experience in Brazil and Mexico shows.

PLENTY is a seasonal crop in Ocara, a parched district of Ceara, a state in Brazil's north-east. Most of its inhabitants piece together a living from odd jobs and family gardens until September, when the annual harvest of cashew nuts brings relief like a long-awaited rain. Recently, the contrast between fat months and lean ones has become less marked, for Ocara's poorest citizens are now drawing a year-round stipend from the government. It is not much, 120 reais ($52) a month at most for a family of five or more. But for Maria Rita Albino da Silva, a "farmer" and cheerful mother of two, it makes the difference between too little food and enough.

Mrs da Silva, along with most of Ocara's population, is a beneficiary of Bolsa Familia ("family fund"), a scheme set up in 2003 that provides a basic income to 7.5m of Brazil's poorest families, or 30m people. The goal is to reach all with a monthly income per head of less than 100 reais—11.2m families, or about a quarter of the population—by the end of next year. The success of Bolsa Familia is almost as vital to Brazil's left-wing president, Luiz Inacio Lula da Silva, as the cash is to Mrs da Silva (no relation). Lula, himself born poor in the north-east, casts himself as a crusader against poverty and corruption. But his government is mired in a party-financing scandal and its first stab at fighting poverty was "Zero Hunger", a feeding programme ridiculed as outmoded and inefficient. Bolsa Familia, officially part of Zero Hunger, is a chance for redemption.

Cash with Strings Attached

It is the biggest of a new generation of social programmes across Latin America, known as "conditional cash transfer" schemes (CCTs). The aim is to alleviate today's poverty, in Brazil's case by transferring up to 95 reais a month to poor families (which states and districts can top up, as Ceara does), and to short-circuit tomorrow's, by making the transfers conditional: beneficiaries must have their children vaccinated, and their health monitored, and keep them in school.

Although CCTs are a Brazilian invention, the first large-scale programme began in Mexico. Originally called Progresa and now

Oportunidades, it now provides government cash transfers to 5m Mexican families, or nearly a quarter of the population. As in Brazil, there are conditions attached. The payments are made every two months, to female heads of household. One element, of around $10 per month, is to help with food. A larger element is to help buy school supplies and pay for transport to and from school. If a child misses more than 15% of class days, or fails a grade twice, these payments are suspended. The payments are also made conditional on the family's regular visits to health clinics.

Comparing Programs in Latin America

Similar schemes now exist in half a dozen Latin American countries, though the details vary. For example, Argentina's programme, expanded to cope with mass unemployment that followed the economy's collapse in 2001–02, has fewer conditions, higher benefits and has been in part sub-contracted to political leaders. By contrast, the Chilean scheme is the only one to focus specifically on the very poorest, and involves much input from social workers who try to ensure that beneficiaries make use of a range of social programmes.

Some Latin American governments spend too little to make any serious dent in poverty and social disadvantage (Brazil and Uruguay are exceptions). Worse, most of what they have spent has been on social insurance. This goes disproportionately to the better off. Compared even with most social assistance schemes, the CCTs are much more closely targeted to the poor. They are not confined to those with formal-sector jobs, which would largely exclude the poor, says Kathy Lindert of the World Bank. The fiscal cost is relatively modest: Brazil's Bolsa Familia costs the federal government 0.36% of GDP [gross domestic product], far less than social insurance schemes. Not only do the poor get cash, but an incentive to use government services. Prior to Oportunidades, says John Scott of CIDE, a university in Mexico City, it was the middle class that would take advantage of health services, rather than the poor. Now poor people go to the doctor more than in the past.

Institutionalizing the Safety Net

Traditionally, too, each government in Latin America has torn up its predecessor's social programmes. No longer. In Mexico, when

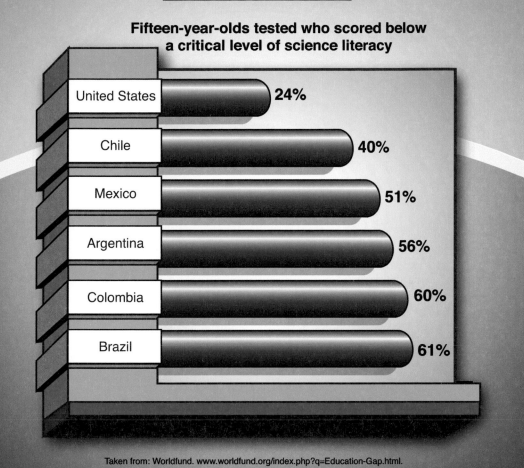

Science Literacy

Fifteen-year-olds tested who scored below a critical level of science literacy

Country	Percentage
United States	24%
Chile	40%
Mexico	51%
Argentina	56%
Colombia	60%
Brazil	61%

Taken from: Worldfund. www.worldfund.org/index.php?q=Education-Gap.html.

Vicente Fox's government took office in 2000, its officials were sceptical of Progresa, which covered 2m rural families that year. But the politicians were convinced by the technocrats—whom Gladys Lopez Acevedo of the World Bank describes as exceptionally skilled. The programme not only survived, but was expanded, both to urban areas and in size. This new social safety-net has thus been "successfully institutionalised", as Ms Lopez Acevedo notes.

In Brazil, when Lula took office in 2003 he inherited a clutch of CCTs spread across various ministries, with different lists of beneficiaries and conditions. His accomplishment has been to turn these into a single, expanded programme while improving their quality. "We didn't start from zero," says Patrus Ananias, the minister of social development, giving the previous government more credit than is customary among Lula's officials. "We integrated and consolidated" the earlier CCTs and pushed up the value of the benefit.

Effective Administration Is Key

The success of the new schemes turns on effective administration. In Mexico, a visit to a government office is normally a far from efficient process. Simple tasks, like getting a driving licence, can take hours in apparently overstaffed offices. By contrast, in an Oportunidades regional office in Apan, a town of 40,000 people in the state of Hidalgo, it takes less than ten seconds for each woman in a queue which snakes out into the street to pick up her allotment of cash. Communities line up in turn. As names are called, each woman appears before the window with an identity card and a difficult-to-forge holographic stamp. All this would have been impossible without computerisation, notes Rodrigo Garcia-Verdu, a researcher at Mexico's central bank. The ability to crunch numbers on a massive scale, he says, is part of what has allowed the programme to be better than any previous social spending in reaching the people it is intended to reach. It also has made it possible to evaluate the effects. . . .

FAST FACT

The percentage of school-aged children enrolled in secondary education is 70 percent in Chile, 56 percent in Mexico, and 15 percent in Brazil.

In Brazil—whose unruly federal structure encompasses 5,561 autonomous municipal districts, ranging from rural outposts like Ocara to the metropolis of Sao Paulo—setting up Bolsa Familia has been far from simple. At first Lula produced confusion rather than consolidation. He created two anti-poverty ministries and yet another CCT. Under a storm of criticism, the government rethought. Four CCTs were merged into Bolsa Familia (a fifth is soon to join). Mr Ananias's ministry was created to run it, replacing the two stillborn ministries. The transition, unsurprisingly, was "chaotic", says an official involved. Quality control was forgotten. Government auditors and the media found fraud in the distribution of benefits and laxity in the monitoring of conditions. With millions of beneficiaries joining the rolls and benefits tripling to an average of 65 reais, Bolsa Familia looked like a blatant bid for popularity rather than serious social policy.

With a new team of career bureaucrats in charge and advice from the World Bank, which is lending $572m to help expand and improve the programme, Bolsa Familia is righting itself. That means fine-tuning an elaborate system in which federal agencies, municipalities, NGO [nongovernmental organization]s and the beneficiaries themselves all play a part.

Using a Single Registry

The task starts with accurate targeting and identification of the beneficiaries. At a church hall in Ocara on a recent Friday the pews were filled with women. They came to enrol in the "single registry" of potential beneficiaries, which replaces the separate rolls of earlier schemes. Three registrars hired by the municipality asked each of the women their family incomes and details such as whether or not their houses had plumbing. But it is the ministry in Brasilia that will decide which of them deserves Bolsa Familia. As in Mexico, women are preferred because they are more likely than their husbands to spend the money on their children. Those who qualify draw benefits from the local branch of a government bank through an electronic card.

With a single registry of potential beneficiaries, the government can check them against its data on employees in the formal sector of the economy. That exercise, conducted for the first time this year, will result in 50,000 people losing their benefits, says Rosani Cunha, who manages Bolsa Familia. District quotas for beneficiaries, which fostered favouritism, have been dropped; now anyone below a certain income level can register, though they may not qualify for a benefit. Under new contracts with the federal government, municipalities must establish "social councils" composed of local officials and representatives of NGOs to monitor implementation. They will also gain more leeway to block and unblock benefits. Municipalities will get federal money to keep the register up to date.

Incentives and Evaluations

The government is driving a harder bargain with beneficiaries, as well. An earlier programme, Bolsa Escola, offered families 15 reais per child for keeping up to three children in school; now all of a family's children must attend classes. Under Bolsa Escola, just 19% of schools reported that children from beneficiary families were regularly attending classes; now 79% do, according to Ms Cunha. The ministry is readying a scale of sanctions, culminating in the total withdrawal of benefits, to promote compliance.

Another advantage of Bolsa Familia, say its boosters, is that objective criteria for conceding benefits are supplanting what Brazilians call "clientelism"—the doling out of favours by local potentates in return for political loyalty. In Ocara, these claims ring true, partly because the long-time mayor, who had governed for most of the district's 19-year history, lost an election last year. According to the local manager of Bolsa Familia, Maria de Sousa Brasil, the re-registration at the church hall will weed out the 20–30% of beneficiaries who were enrolled undeservedly by the old regime.

The evidence from Mexico, where more evaluation has been done, is that CCTs do work. A June 2004 paper in the *Journal of the American Medical Association* found improvements in the size and health of children participating in the programme. Drop-out rates among secondary-school students are also down—by roughly 5% for boys and 8% for girls, according to a study by Paul Schultz of Yale University. That may be an underestimate: a simulation done by Jere Behrman and his colleagues at the Penn Institute for Economic Research in Philadelphia suggests that Oportunidades could increase secondary-school enrolment by 19%.

Cash Transfers Only Part of Solution

On their own, the cash-transfer schemes can alleviate but not abolish poverty. Even Oportunidades does not reach the poorest of Mexico's rural poor, who live in communities so small that they do not have schools or health clinics within reach—a number that Mr Scott estimates at 500,000 people. Secondly, getting more children to attend school is only as effective as the schools themselves. Mexico spends a fairly large percentage of GDP on education, but its students still lag

Argentina's Conditional Cash Transfer Program was instituted following the country's economic collapse in 2002. Similar programs now exist in six other Latin American countries.

badly on standardised tests. The same goes for Brazil. Schools that Ocara's education secretary calls "apathetic" are unlikely to teach much, even if students stay until age 15, as Bolsa Familia requires.

Thirdly, cash transfers might generate some jobs, but in Ocara locals say that employment will come only when water does, and that depends on investment by the hard-pressed federal government. Indeed, according to Ms de Sousa Brasil, some beneficiaries stop working entirely, content to live off the benefit, meagre though it is. Avoiding such dependence will require further changes to Bolsa

Familia. There is talk of "complementary programmes" to shepherd people into productive work, a strong point of Chile's programme. Teenagers could get bonuses for graduating from school, as they do in Mexico, rather than dropping out after their benefits expire, as happens now. There is more to be done in co-ordinating federal, state and local programmes. It will be a long time before Ocara blooms year-round. But a start has been made.

EVALUATING THE AUTHOR'S ARGUMENTS:

The author contends that CCTs encourage school attendance and utilization of health services, but does the author establish that CCTs reduce poverty? Give reasons for your answer.

Conditional Transfer Payments Will Not Reduce Poverty

Heather Mac Donald

"Cash rewards for conduct that is simply part of what it means to be a conscientious parent or student is no way to inculcate a more functional value system."

Heather Mac Donald argues in this viewpoint that conditional cash transfers, tied to behaviors such as school attendance or seeking medical care, will not reduce poverty. While she agrees that changing the behavior of the poor is necessary to reduce poverty, she says that giving them money to do so will make the problem worse, not better. People should be responsible out of a sense of duty, the author contends, not because they are paid to do so. Mac Donald is a contributing editor to the Manhattan Institute's *City Journal*.

AS YOU READ, CONSIDER THE FOLLOWING QUESTIONS:

1. Under the plan discussed by the author, what would a parent be paid to review his or her child's school test scores?
2. In the view of the author, why do the poor fail to plan for the future?
3. In what country do defenders of the program say conditional cash transfers have worked, as stated by Mac Donald?

N ew York mayor Michael Bloomberg announced his latest change of political party two weeks ago [in June 2007] and cast himself as an innovative anti-politician. "Any success-ful elected executive knows that real results are more important than partisan battles," he said via press release, "and that good ideas should take precedence over rigid adherence to any particular political ideol-ogy." Such results-oriented executives, the implication was clear, are precisely what presidential voters are hungering for.

By now, there are few political appeals more conventional than the claim that one is unconventional and above party. But this time, the newly minted independent mayor (who had just lightly dispensed with his temporary and self-serving "Republican" identity) had rolled out a "new" solution to an old problem—poverty—the day before. Anyone interested in seeing what Bloomberg's rhetoric of "innova-tive," nonpartisan problem-solving means in practice will find his new poverty plan illuminating. It combines a clever technocratic veneer with a profound ignorance of civil society. If this at present privately funded pilot were ever duplicated widely, it could prove to be one of the most destructive welfare policies ever devised.

Bloomberg plans to pay low-income parents in six New York neigh-borhoods to behave responsibly toward their children, and their chil-dren to take advantage of school. Starting in September 2007, 2,550 parents enrolled in the "Opportunity NYC conditional cash transfer" pilot will get $25 for reviewing their child's test scores, and another $25 for discussing those scores with a teacher. Merely attending a parent-teacher conference earns $25. Obtaining a library card nets $50; taking one's child to the dentist or to a doctor-recommended (and taxpayer-subsidized) medical exam, $100. Students will receive monthly bounties for school attendance; improvement on standard-ized tests yields about $300; completing 11 high-school credits is priced at $600 a year. In a separate pilot, 9,000 fourth- and seventh-grade students will receive up to $100 simply for taking required math and English tests; answering all questions correctly garners up to $500.

Funding for the $53 million pilot is to come from foundations such as Rockefeller and George Soros's Open Society Institute, as well as from Mayor Bloomberg himself. But if after two years the project architects are satisfied with the results, the mayor envisages extending the incentives city-wide and paying for them with hundreds of millions of tax dollars.

Cash for Good Behavior

Give the Bloomberg policymakers credit for one thing: The cash-for-responsibility plan violates the greatest taboo in the poverty industry. It implicitly recognizes that the long-term poor are held back more by their own behavior than by social inequities. Talk to any inner-city teacher and you will hear how difficult it is to get parents involved in their child's education, or students to bother with homework. Countless schemes for tutoring and job training sit on the shelves unused because the "clients" never show up. Free medical advice is wasted because patients don't return for follow-up visits, if they bother following the doctor's instructions at all. After the urban riots of the 1960s, political scientist Edward Banfield observed that the central trait separating the poor from the prosperous is future orientation. His insight has never been improved upon. The middle and upper classes defer gratification and invest effort in self-improvement,

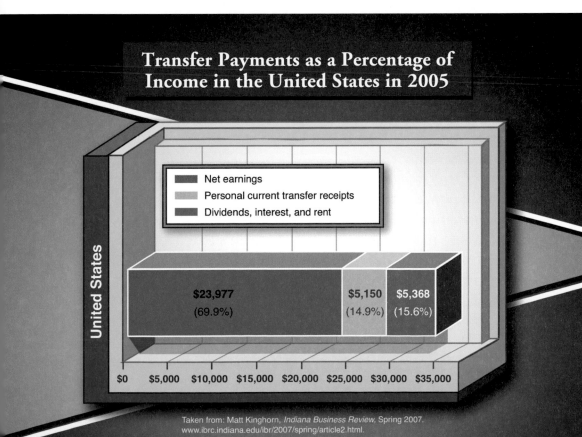

Transfer Payments as a Percentage of Income in the United States in 2005

Net earnings
Personal current transfer receipts
Dividends, interest, and rent

United States

$23,977
(69.9%)

$5,150
(14.9%)

$5,368
(15.6%)

$0 $5,000 $10,000 $15,000 $20,000 $25,000 $30,000 $35,000

Taken from: Matt Kinghorn, *Indiana Business Review*, Spring 2007.
www.ibrc.indiana.edu/ibr/2007/spring/article2.html.

The author argues that New York City mayor Michael Bloomberg's privately funded poverty program, announced in 2002, is one of the most destructive welfare policies ever devised.

Banfield wrote in *The Unheavenly City: The Nature and Future of our Urban Crisis;* were the underclass to do so, they would not long stay in the bottom economic tier.

In unveiling his "conditional cash transfer" scheme on June 18, Bloomberg predictably eschewed Banfield's bracing honesty. The poor fail to "plan for the future," the mayor said, because they are "so focused on surviving." The idea that the residents of Brooklyn and Central Harlem are engaged in a "struggle," as Bloomberg put it, against starvation and depredation is a fantasy. Many teens who will be enrolled in "Opportunity NYC" likely wear the latest sneakers and carry pagers and cell phones. Their problem is motivation, not the unforgiving demands of a subsistence economy. Nevertheless,

Bloomberg should be congratulated for implicitly acknowledging the behavior issue, however misleading the rhetoric in which he couches it.

Cure Worse than the Disease

But the cure in this case will be worse than the disease. Introducing cash rewards for conduct that is simply part of what it means to be a conscientious parent or student is no way to inculcate a more functional value system. Creating the expectation of immediate cash for behavior that provides a long-term payoff, such as studying in school, will further shorten the poor's time horizon, rather than lengthen it. Civil society requires individuals to undertake countless actions in the private sphere out of a sense of duty and propriety. The state cannot possibly devise a payment schedule complex enough to capture those actions, nor should it try.

Liberal supporters of the Bloomberg payment plan claim that conservatives should love it—after all, it involves money, doesn't it? And we all know that the only thing conservatives care about is money and the market. But the market is made up of entities and individuals involved in discretionary, profit-seeking transactions. There should be nothing discretionary about encouraging your child's education or providing him with medical care (especially when that care is free). These behaviors are moral obligations, not economic exchanges. Nor are the "conditional cash transfers" comparable to tax incentives for corporate investment, for the same reason: Tax breaks, rightly or wrongly, aim to influence optional spending.

FAST FACT

Transfer payments as a percentage of income in the United States have increased from under 7 percent in 1965 to nearly 15 percent in 2005.

"But the program works in Mexico," say its defenders. Leaving aside whether Mexican poverty policy cries out for emulation, Mexican peasants are facing a "struggle" for subsistence, unlike America's inner-city poor. A campesina's decision to take her child to the doctor may in fact jeopardize her livelihood, making the $200 offset, for example, which the Bloomberg administration intends to pay parents simply for taking their child to an annual medical check-up, a significant cushion against risk. New York is a different universe. The Bloomberg plan will pay parents $40 a month merely for maintaining taxpayer subsidized health insurance—the barrier to doing which is apathy and inertia, not a Dickensian struggle for survival.

The Case Against Bribery

Should the Bloomberg payment experiment go large-scale, as its architects hope, it will create a bizarre caste system, in which one part of society bribes the other to behave in ways that the paying class regards as basic to responsible human life. So far, the Bloomberg administration has not articulated any principle for distinguishing who is in that paying class, and who in the payee class, other than a crude income test. The program will enroll families at or below 130 percent of the federal poverty level. How will the administration explain to parents at 140 percent of the federal poverty line that their children should attend school simply because it is in their long-term self-interest, when their neighbors are getting paid for the same behavior?

Nor has City Hall said what its end game is. Once the payments are institutionalized, it will be difficult to dislodge the expectations that they create. Welfare advocates are already arguing that the bounties are not large enough. Expect a constant push from the poverty industry to raise the price of good behavior, to broaden the payee class, and to compensate a greater range of conduct—making sure that one's child has had breakfast or takes his books to school would seem to be as worthy of being remunerated as downloading a child's test scores. And once word gets around classrooms that some students are taking home $500 for doing well on tests, good luck persuading other students that they should study for the love of learning or the prospect of a better future.

Throughout his mayoralty, Bloomberg has pursued conventional liberal solutions to poverty, going on an affordable-housing building spree, for example, and seeking to water down the work requirements in welfare reform. His latest endeavor at least breaks with that conventional wisdom by correctly diagnosing the behavioral roots of entrenched poverty. Its remedy is blind, however, to the moral basis of civil society. If Bloomberg really wants to earn the title of independent, he should promote marriage as a way of reducing poverty. Now that would be a radical idea.

EVALUATING THE AUTHOR'S ARGUMENTS:

Does the author demonstrate that conditional transfer payments will not promote the desired behavior changes or reduce poverty? What harm does the author say will result from conditional transfer payments?

Economic Freedom Reduces Poverty

"Poverty is escaped when the small economic interactions expand into more efficient enterprises."

Kimani S. Njoroge

Kimani S. Njoroge argues in this viewpoint that economic freedom reduces poverty. The author contends that market-friendly environments, which are characterized by minimum government regulation, promote economic activity that creates prosperity for all. The success of economic freedom in bringing about prosperity is a truth that the author says applies to all nations. Njoroge is a research fellow at the Foundation for Economic Education.

AS YOU READ, CONSIDER THE FOLLOWING QUESTIONS:

1. What percentage of Uganda's government spending is foreign aid, according to statistics cited by the author?
2. According to rankings cited by Njoroge, what African country has the freest economy, and how much did it reduce poverty between 1990 and 2006?
3. How did Tanzania's poverty level change during the same period, and to what does the author attribute the change?

Kimani S. Njoroge, "Reducing Poverty Through Economic Freedom," Foundation for Economic Education, June 6, 2008. Reproduced by permission.

T he worldwide obsession with poverty eradication is a major threat to economic freedom in developing nations. Through central planning, governments and aid agencies are busy blocking poor people's road to prosperity. The United Nations Millennium Development Goals (MDGs)—which seeks to magically reduce worldwide poverty by half before 2015—is the most popular, and disastrous, plan. The MDG Secretariat is urging developed countries to double their foreign aid, which will be used to promote UN programs on extreme hunger; primary education; gender equality; child mortality; maternal health; HIV/AIDS, malaria, and other diseases; environmental sustainability; and global partnership for development. The UN claims that poverty would be history if those issues were addressed. But it ain't so! Things would be worse, considering that poor nations are being encouraged to spend more on the aforementioned programs. This would widen avenues of corruption and increase budget imbalances, both of which have crippled Third World economies for decades.

Market-Friendly Environments Needed

Then enter the Bretton Woods Poverty Reduction Strategy Papers (PRSP) that developing nations must submit as requisites for foreign aid and debt relief. In these papers governments are required to describe their "countries' macroeconomic and structural policies to be used in the promotion of broad-based growth and poverty reduction," as well as indicating the amount of foreign aid needed. Failure to submit convincing PRSPs is suicidal to countries like Uganda, where foreign aid accounts for over 50 percent of government spending. This means empowering seasoned bureaucrats with the task of developing these nations' master plans

FAST FACT

Countries in the top fifth of economic freedom have incomes nine times that of countries in the bottom fifth of economic freedom.

against poverty. William Easterly, author of *The White Man's Burden*, wonders why such powers are given to bureaucrats, instead of to individuals who actually reduce poverty through enterprise.

The resulting economic policies end up appeasing donor agencies at the cost of robbing poor folks of opportunities to help themselves. Their strong emphasis on ending poverty through welfare programs and intergovernmental transfers is creating a mentality that governments exist not to preserve liberty but rather to improve lives through tax money and donor funds. Thus instead of pushing for institutional reforms that would confine governments to protecting life, liberty, and property, and providing market-friendly environments, Third World civil societies are pushing for more transparency and accountability in their nations' wealth-transfer systems. Their goal is to make governments behave like flawless conduits of distribution. But that will never happen; government planning will only prevent the establishment of long-run market solutions to poverty.

Reduced Government Promotes Economic Freedom

Two independent projects (one by the Cato and Fraser Institutes and the other by the Heritage Foundation and *Wall Street Journal*) have consistently found that economic prosperity is greater in countries whose governments stick to the role of protecting life, liberty, and property. These findings confirm Frederic Bastiat's claim in *The Law* that economically prosperous people are to be found in:

> countries where the law least interferes with private affairs; where government is least felt; where the individual has the greatest scope, and free opinion the greatest influence; where administrative powers are fewest and simplest; where taxes are lightest and most nearly equal, and popular discontent the least excited and the least justifiable; where individuals and groups most actively assume their responsibilities, and, consequently, where the morals of admittedly imperfect human beings are constantly improving; where trade, assemblies, and associations are the least restricted; where labor, capital, and populations suffer the fewest forced displacements; where mankind most nearly follows its own natural inclinations; where the inventions of men are most nearly in harmony with the laws of God.

A Ugandan woman and her children in a government refugee camp wait for assistance. Uganda has East Africa's freest economy and has reduced its abject poverty level from 56 percent to 37.7 percent in recent years.

Economic Freedom Is Universal Panacea

The success of economic freedom in bringing forth prosperity holds true for all nations. Comparing three neighboring East African countries (Kenya, Uganda, and Tanzania) tells it all. Two decades of different levels of economic freedom have produced different economic fortunes in these countries. According to the 2007 Human Development Report, Uganda, reported to be East Africa's freest economy by the Heritage rankings, has managed to reduce abject poverty from 56 percent of the population in 1990 to 37.7 percent in 2006. The country has continued to sustain the region's highest annual per capita productivity ($1,478), highest life expectancy (48.4 yrs), and highest education enrollment ratio (66.1 percent). Kenya, second after Uganda in economic freedom, comes second in all measures; her abject-poverty rate rose from a little more than four points (from 48 percent in 1990 to 52.2 percent in 2006). Annual per capita productivity currently stands at $1,140, life expectancy at 47.5 years, and the education

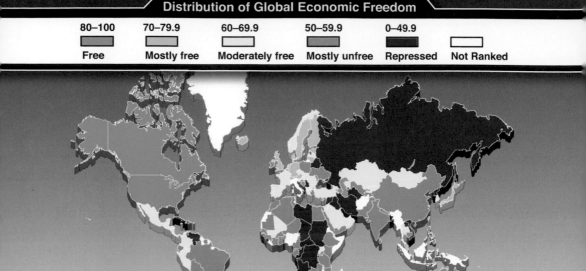

Distribution of Global Economic Freedom

80–100	70–79.9	60–69.9	50–59.9	0–49.9	
Free	Mostly free	Moderately free	Mostly unfree	Repressed	Not Ranked

Taken from: American Heritage Foundation. www.heritage.org/research/features/index/countries.cfm.

enrollment ratio at 60.1 percent. Tanzania, with the least economic freedom of the trio, lags in all measures: its abject-poverty rate rose by 7 points (from 28 percent in 1990 to 35.7 percent in 2006), per capita productivity stands at $674, and life expectancy at 45.9 years. The country has a sorry education enrollment ratio of 47.1 percent.

The Ugandan example is testament that free people can indeed pull themselves up from poverty. The scale of their economic activities does not matter, as long as they want to improve their lives through the best means they know—whether as subsistence farmers or micro-entrepreneurs. Nobel laureate Milton Friedman referred to them as a collection of Robinson Crusoes who cooperate in the production of goods and services.

Economic Freedom Provides Solution Through Development

Poverty is escaped when the small economic interactions expand into more efficient enterprises. This is aided by the existence of strong market-friendly environments that Cato and Fraser describe as better protection of private property, proper enhancement of contract laws, stable monetary environment, low taxes, elimination of trade barriers, and the allocation of goods and resources through the market process. But instead of providing that, governments, especially in developing nations, regard rising enterprises as sources of revenue to be milked through business licenses, fees, and taxes. Farmers are seen as time-wasters who cannot succeed without government help and who thus are coerced into selling their commodities through government marketing boards. Such boards helped wreck coffee farming in Kenya, cocoa in Ghana, and tobacco in Malawi. Small traders are seen as economic nuisances who need to be eliminated altogether. Such interventions end up destabilizing small-scale enterprises that already account for huge portions of these nations' economic output.

To reverse that trend, economic freedom needs to be seen as a development partner. Governments must understand that providing market-friendly environments will enable their societies to develop long-lasting solutions to economic problems and, as Friedman wrote in *Capitalism and Freedom*, "reduce the range of issues that must be resolved through [ineffective] political means."

EVALUATING THE AUTHOR'S ARGUMENTS:

The author cites the experience of Uganda in support of his argument, yet foreign aid accounts for a large percentage of Uganda's government spending. Does this fact contradict or support the author's argument? Give reasons for your answer.

The Press Should Report More on Poverty

E.J. Dionne Jr., interviewed by Mary Ellen Schoonmaker

"Poverty is a problem that should be discussed nationally."

In this viewpoint Mary Ellen Schoonmaker interviews E.J. Dionne Jr., who argues that the press should report more on poverty. The media, he argues, is biased against reporting on poverty because it is geared to reporting on issues that interest the wealthy. Dionne contends that the poor have compelling stories to which many can relate. Stories about the connection poverty has to other issues affecting the community, he maintains, are important to all economic groups. Schoonmaker is an editorial board member at *The Record*. Dionne is a columnist and political writer for the *Washington Post*.

AS YOU READ, CONSIDER THE FOLLOWING QUESTIONS:

1. As reported by Dionne, what phrase did Jim Wallis coin to refer to a category of poor voters?
2. Why, in Dionne's view, can those who are not poor relate to stories about the poor?
3. What issues affecting the entire community does Dionne say poverty has an effect on?

Mary Ellen Schoonmaker, "Keeping Poverty on the Page: Covering an Old Problem in New Ways," *Columbia Journalism Review,* January 1, 2008. Reproduced by permission of the publisher and the author.

*M*ary Ellen Schoonmaker: How can local reporters, who are not on the [campaign] trail . . . link what some of the candidates are saying about poverty to coverage in their own back yards?

E.J. Dionne: People talk all the time about media bias. I actually think there's a structural bias in the media against the poor. Newspapers are built to cover the wealthy and the famous much more than they are built to cover the working class or the poor. There are entire business sections devoted to what the people running big companies do. There are whole sections that focus on gossip about celebrities and rich sports figures. There are good reasons why all these sections exist, but taken together, this is a very large commitment on the part of journalists to a particular slice of society. There is no part of the newspaper routinely devoted to the coverage of the problems of poor people, or struggling working-class—or even middle-class—people. So anyone who cares about covering these matters knows he or she has to fight this structural issue. That said, a lot of these stories are very compelling stories. Jim Wallis, the progressive evangelical, invented a whole category of voters from a visit to a Burger King where he saw a mom working behind the counter while two of her kids were doing their homework. He called her a "Burger King mom." She was doing everything society said she should because we don't provide universal childcare, and because people in lower-end service jobs don't have flexibility with their time—there were her kids doing their homework. I think the stories of folks like that are very compelling to readers. I think stories illustrating what these numbers about the lack of health-care coverage mean, or what the imposition of higher co-pays or insurance costs mean to actual people, are compelling stories. I have been a political reporter for a long time, and this critique applies as much to me as to anyone else. We probably don't do enough to take these abstract issues and explain them in light of people's actual experiences. And I think that can be done at every newspaper in the country, and indeed reporters on local papers may be in a position to do a better job of this than those of us so focused on the horse race of the [2008] presidential election.

Community Should Think About Poverty

Given this "structural bias," what can one reporter—or one editor—do to fight it?

Journalism is rooted in the faith that a single reporter can make a difference. It often happens in the case of stories about political or financial corruption and in stories calling attention to serious public problems that have been ignored. I think it's possible for a reporter to encourage a community to give more thought to issues related to poverty, and perhaps to think about them differently. It's important to make a case that there is a "but for the grace of God go I" aspect to many of these stories. Readers who are not poor can relate especially to stories in which they could imagine themselves if their luck ran out, or if they were born into different circumstances. And because many people these days who aren't poor feel under various financial pressures, there are ways to link their situations to the situations of the poor.

Can you do it in a way that doesn't make people feel guilty, or that they have heard it all before?

Maybe this just proves that I'm Catholic, but I don't think there's anything wrong with making people feel guilty; I think we should have a sense of guilt or, if you prefer, a responsibility about this suffering in our midst. In terms of whether this turns people off, there are books that have been best-sellers that call our attention to this. One thinks of the classic, *The Other America*, by Michael Harrington, which had an enormous effect in making us pay attention to the poor. There are Barbara Ehrenreich's books [such as *Nickel and Dimed*] that were very compelling to a lot of people. So I don't think this coverage turns people off, nor does it all have to be downbeat. A lot of stories about the poor are heroic stories of people who despite the odds are trying to do the right thing. There's a problem when poor people get in the paper more for committing crimes than for doing the right thing.

Dialogue About Poverty Is Important

How do we do it in a way that doesn't feed this attitude that the poor are somehow to blame for their plight?

I don't see anything wrong with explaining that poverty is very complicated and that there is personal responsibility here as well as the social problems and racism that are involved in creating poverty. If you take some of the great writers, recently, about poverty—I think of Alex Kotlowitz or Jason DeParle—they're really honest about the

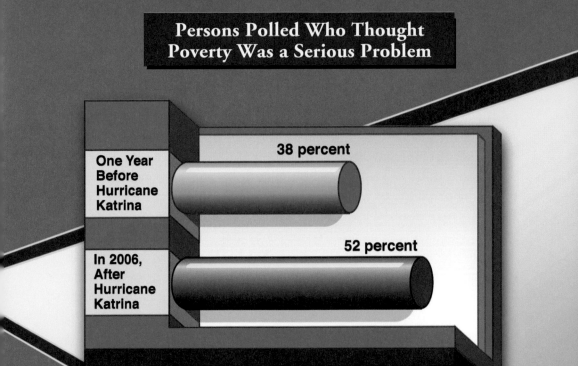

Persons Polled Who Thought Poverty Was a Serious Problem

One Year Before Hurricane Katrina — 38 percent

In 2006, After Hurricane Katrina — 52 percent

Taken from: Fairness and Accuracy in Reporting, September/October 2007.

complexity of this; that poor people make mistakes just like everyone else. The breakdown of the family is a real problem that we shouldn't shy away from covering. It shouldn't be done in a propagandistic way, but in a way that calls the public's attention to these problems and makes them part of the larger dialogue. The person who covers poverty right most consistently and I think courageously is Bob Herbert of *The New York Times*.

But don't you think that this dialogue about the poor has been largely diminished in recent years, that since 9/11, national attention has turned toward a very insular defense of "us against them"?

I think there are fads and vogues in journalism; there always have been. I think there are moments when certain stories push their way up front, and often for good reason. It made perfect sense after 9/11 to have the media spend an awful lot of time on terrorism. But things change and people go back to, or forward to, other interests, and I think Americans still care about the story of terrorism, but I don't think this drives all the coverage, or for that matter all our politics, anymore. I also think that we have to be candid that what journalists do is in many ways reactive to what is happening in the political environment, and I think it's been awhile since people in our political realm were willing to push poverty up front, particularly in a presidential campaign. The late Paul Wellstone [the senator from Minnesota], before he died, tried to do it with his poverty tour, where he retraced Bobby Kennedy's steps. Certainly John Edwards has made this a major theme of his [2008 presidential] campaign, and I think Barack Obama and Hillary Clinton are doing that to a degree—both have given serious poverty speeches. And in Congress, with the S-CHIP debate, for example, the state children's health-insurance program, you're opening up on a national level, day after day after day, a debate about how poor and lower-middle-class and middle-class kids get, or do not get, health care. So I think the environment now is more conducive to real coverage of these problems and this issue than it was just two or three years ago.

Katrina Generated Outrage About Poverty

There was a compelling series recently in The Buffalo News *that explored the story behind new census figures that show Buffalo is the second-poorest large city in America, and almost half its children live in poverty. What does it mean to go to bed hungry, to be hungry when you get home from school and there's nothing to eat? The paper focused on individual children to humanize the issue. It was powerful stuff, but then they interviewed the mayor, and he said something like, Oh, yes, we've got all these projects in the pipeline, and we're developing, and we're going to come back as a city, etc., and it ultimately left me unsatisfied. Will anything change? Where is the outrage? Should journalism be more willing to tell people that they should be angry about situations like this?*

You know the one place where you did see that happen was Hurricane Katrina. It is true that after a burst of interest in the chronic poverty that Katrina exposed there is much less interest now, much less coverage of what is happening down there. But I, like a lot of people, was struck at how visibly angry reporters on the ground got about how people were being treated. It really was almost a muckraking style, and it wasn't ideological; it was just, there's a human outrage here. I do think that in the period immediately after 9/11, there was a kind of patriotic style of coverage, and I understand that, because we all felt that the United States was under attack, and there was a sense of solidarity in the country. But that cannot dominate journalism for long without journalism having a problem, and I think you're seeing a move again toward a more critical style of coverage.

Politicians Beginning to See Poverty as an Issue

But wasn't the much-praised Katrina coverage actually an anomaly?
Katrina was powerful because it combined a huge natural disaster (such stories always get covered) with a huge social catastrophe. Social catastrophes get far less coverage. So it is not surprising that Katrina was the exception. But again, I think we should be candid about vogues in journalism, how a whole series of factors can come together to create an interest in a topic. In the early 1960s, it was the combination of John F. Kennedy campaigning in West Virginia and seeing how much poverty there was, and Dwight MacDonald's review of Mike Harrington's book in *The New Yorker* that came to Kennedy's attention, and Lyndon Johnson's own moral sense about poverty

FAST FACT

Between September 11, 2003, and October 30, 2006, a total of only fifty-eight stories related to poverty appeared on *ABC World News, NBC Nightly News,* or *CBS Evening News.*

and the civil-rights movement, which moved from a focus on the rights of African Americans to the opportunities, or lack thereof, that all African Americans had. So you had a whole lot of factors coming together. I think now what you have coming together is obviously Hurricane Katrina, a sense on the part of some politicians at least that poverty is a problem that should be discussed nationally, and a real concern among the middle class about rising inequality and what it means for the country and for democracy, and that their own circumstances are more fragile than they should be.

Poverty Reporting Need Not Be Advocacy

The Buffalo News *series was not about advocacy. Its role was to "be the spotlight on the problem, not an actor on the stage." Does this surprise you?*

Washington Post *columnist E.J. Dionne Jr. says that the poor have more compelling and newsworthy stories than the rich and famous, and the press should cover the plight of the poor more.*

On the one hand, because I care about these issues, I would love to see the paper crusade. On the other hand, I think there is something very valuable about saying, "We're not going to dictate how you look at this." There is a case to be made for good reporting that is not linked to advocacy. Yes, editorial pages are supposed to advocate, but I think a lot of people never believe you when you say that the editorial side of the paper is independent of the news side, when at the vast majority of papers it actually is.

Because most reporters are middle class, like our readers, are there biases that we bring—blind spots—that get in our way when we write about poverty?

My conservative friends say the media are biased, liberal, and in fact I think the bias in the media is one of the educated, middle- to upper-middle class. So if there's a bias on social issues, it's more liberal, but if there's a bias on economic issues, it tends to be slightly conservative. I joke that the two things you don't want to be in confronting a reporter are an evangelical preacher or a trade-union shop steward. Having said that, the best journalists have a kind of empathetic ability, the ability to see the world not just from their own perspective but from somebody else's perspective. At its best, journalism is an interaction between an empathetic view and a critical view, which is: How does the world look from this perspective? And viewed a little bit from the outside, does that perspective make sense or not? Does it always work? No. But when it does, it can produce some great journalism.

Report the Effects of Poverty on Other Issues

What are some aspects of the poverty issue that are under-covered and too important to ignore?

To the extent that poverty is linked to high crime rates, a whole community has an interest in doing something. School failure is a huge issue because it blocks kids from rising out of poverty. School success, by the way, is also important and almost never covered. The impact of poverty on people's health—and the health costs this can impose on a community—is important. We also need a lot more coverage of family breakdown and single-parent families, to figure out more about the connection between family structure and poverty and what can be done about it. It's a problem not easily dealt with through public policy. It's important to show why jobs may be harder to find in inner-city communities than in suburban areas. It's important to show that the poor often lack transportation to travel from where they live to where the jobs are.

Report About Solutions to Poverty

How can a reporter keep the people in a story on poverty from becoming one-dimensional, simply the sum of their problems? Do poverty stories always have to be grim?

Poverty stories don't have to be grim. We don't write often enough about solutions, about programs or agencies that work—and explain to readers why they work. We don't write often enough about people who work with the poor. There are many religious organizations that do amazing work, and whose commitment is something many in a community can relate to. There are affluent churches and synagogues that partner with houses of worship in less-affluent parts of their communities. These are often settings in which the well-off and the less well-off relate to each other in human ways, and not as "caregivers" and "clients." And the poor often have a sense of humor about their own condition, which can create a spark of recognition in readers.

> ### EVALUATING THE AUTHOR'S ARGUMENTS:
>
> The author claims that there is a structural bias in the media that favors reporting about the wealthy and famous. Do you believe that this is true from your own experiences? Does the author explain why this is so?

Facts About Poverty

Editor's note: These facts can be used in reports or papers to reinforce or add credibility when making important points or claims.

World Poverty
According to the UN World Food Program, *World Hunger Series, 2007:*
- 2 billion people suffer from hidden hunger or micronutrient deficiencies affecting them even when they consume adequate calories and protein.
- 90 percent of the world's hungry live with chronic hunger—a nagging hunger that does not go away.
- 178 million children under age five are stunted or short in stature due to poor nutrition.
- 143 million children under age five are underweight in developing countries; of those, 121 million live in low-income food-deficient countries.
- 53 percent of childhood deaths have undernutrition as a synergistic cause.
- Only 2.1 million people escape hunger each year, far short of the MDG 1 target.
- 57 percent of malaria deaths are attributable to undernutrition.
- One-third of the 40 million people living with HIV are also infected with tuberculosis.
- 80 percent of chronic diseases occur in low-income and middle-income countries.

U.S. Poverty by Region, State, and City
According to the Catholic Campaign for Human Development, citing information from the U.S. Census Bureau 2006 and American Community Survey, 2007:
- The states with the highest poverty rates are Mississippi, 21.1%; District of Columbia, 19.6%; Louisiana, 19.0%; New Mexico,

18.5%; Arkansas, 17.3%; West Virginia, 17.3%; Kentucky, 17.0%; Oklahoma, 17.0%; Texas, 16.9%; and Alabama, 16.6%.

- The top ten states with the most children under age eighteen living in poverty are District of Columbia, 32%; Mississippi, 29.5%; Louisiana, 27.8%; New Mexico, 25.6%; West Virginia, 25.2%; Arkansas, 24.3%; Oklahoma, 24.3%; Texas, 23.9%; Alabama, 23.0%; and Kentucky, 22.8%.
- The top ten states with the most persons sixty-five or older living in poverty are Mississippi, 15.7%; District of Columbia, 15.2%; Louisiana, 13.9%; Kentucky, 13.5%; Tennessee, 13.4%; New Mexico, 13.0%; Alabama, 12.6%; Georgia, 12.6%; South Dakota, 12.5%; Arkansas and Texas, 12.3%.
- Top ten counties (250,000 or more in population) with highest poverty rates are Hidalgo County, TX, 36.9%; Cameron County, TX, 35.9%; Bronx County, NY, 29.1%; El Paso County, TX, 27.7%; St. Louis County, MO, 26.8%; Philadelphia County, PA, 25.1%; Kings County, NY, 22.6%; Caddo Parish, LA, 22.4%; Nueces County, TX, 22.1%; and Tulare County, CA, 21.6%.
- Top ten cities (250,000 or more in population) with highest poverty rates are Detroit, MI, 32.5%; Buffalo, NY, 29.9%; Cincinnati, OH, 27.8%; Cleveland, OH, 27.0%; Miami, FL, 26.9%; St. Louis, MO, 26.8%; El Paso, TX, 26.4%; Milwaukee, WI, 26.2%; Philadelphia, PA, 25.1%; and Newark, NJ, 24.2%.
- Cities of less than 250,000 with highest poverty rates are Brownsville, TX, 40.6%; College Station, TX, 37.3%; Camden, NJ, 35.6%; Edinburg, TX, 35.4%; Bloomington, IN, 34.7%; Flint, MI, 34.1%; Kalamazoo, MI, 33.4%; Florence-Graham CDP, CA, 33.0%; Gary, IN, 32.8%; and Muncie, IN, 32.6%.

Poverty in Africa
According to the organization Food 4 Africa:
- One in two of all people in sub-Saharan Africa—315 million people—survive on less than one dollar per day.
- Thirty-three percent of the African population—184 million people—suffer from malnutrition.
- During the 1990s the average income per capita decreased in twenty African countries.

- Less than 50 percent of Africa's population has access to hospitals or doctors.
- In 2000, 300 million Africans did not have access to safe water.
- The average life expectancy in Africa is forty-one years.
- Only 57 percent of African children are enrolled in primary education, and only one of three children completes school.
- One in six children dies before the age of five. This number is twenty-five times higher in sub-Saharan Africa than in the OECD countries.
- Children account for half of all civilian casualties in wars in Africa.
- The African continent lost more than 5.3 million hectares of forest during the decade of the 1990s.
- Fewer than one person out of five has electricity.

Poverty's Effects on Water and Sanitation
According to the 2006 United Nations Human Development Report:
- 1.1 billion people in developing countries have inadequate access to water.
- 2.2 billion people lack basic sanitation.
- Access to piped water into the household averages about 85 percent for the wealthiest 20 percent of the population compared with 25 percent for the poorest 20 percent.
- 1.8 million children die each year as a result of diarrhea.
- Water-related illness causes a loss of 443 million school days each year.
- Close to half of all persons in developing countries are suffering at any given time with health problems caused by water and sanitation deficits.

Poverty in Southeast Asia
According the World Bank, 2006:
- Approximately half of the world's poor live in Southeast Asia.
- In Southeast Asia 85 percent of people live on less than two dollar per day.
- Southeast Asia has one of the highest illiteracy rates in the world.

Organizations to Contact

The editors have compiled the following list of organizations concerned with the issues debated in this book. The descriptions are derived from materials provided by the organizations. All have publications or information available for interested readers. The list was compiled on the date of publication of the present volume; the information provided here may change. Be aware that many organizations take several weeks or longer to respond to queries, so allow as much time as possible.

Brookings Institution
1775 Massachusetts Ave. NW
Washington, DC 20036-2188
e-mail: brookinfo@brook.edu
Web site: www.brook.edu

The Brookings Institution is a private, nonprofit organization that conducts research on economics, education, foreign and domestic government policy, and the social sciences. It publishes the quarterly *Brookings Review* and many books through its publishing division, the Brookings Institution Press. A searchable database on the Web site provides access to articles on poverty.

CARE USA
151 Ellis St. NE
Atlanta, GA 30303
Web site: www.care.org

CARE is a leading humanitarian organization fighting global poverty, placing special focus upon women. Women are at the heart of CARE's community-based efforts to improve basic education, prevent the spread of HIV, increase access to clean water and sanitation, expand economic opportunity, and protect natural resources. CARE also delivers emergency aid to survivors of war and natural disasters and helps people rebuild their lives. The organization's Web site provides information concerning global poverty.

Catholic Campaign for Human Development
United States Conference of Catholic Bishops
3211 Fourth St. NE
Washington, DC 20017-1194
Web site: www.nccbuscc.org

The National Conference of Catholic Bishops (NCCB) established the Catholic Campaign for Human Development (CCHD), the Catholic Church's domestic antipoverty program, in 1969. Since 1970, CCHD has provided nearly eight thousand grants to self-help projects developed by grassroots groups of poor persons nationwide. Each year CCHD distributes national grants to more than three hundred projects based in local communities. The organization's Web site provides information on poverty and the opportunity to participate in programs that fight poverty.

Cato Institute
1000 Massachusetts Ave. NW
Washington, DC 20001-5403
e-mail: cato@cato.org
Web site: www.cato.org

The Cato Institute is a libertarian public policy research foundation dedicated to limiting the role of government and protecting individual liberties. The Cato Institute is named after *Cato's Letters*, a series of libertarian pamphlets that Cato's founders say helped lay the philosophical foundation for the American Revolution. Cato's searchable database allows access to a number of articles on poverty and its causes, presented from a libertarian perspective.

Center for Global Development
1776 Massachusetts Ave. NW, 3rd Fl.
Washington, DC 20036
(202) 416-0700
Web site: www.cgdev.org

This organization is an independent, not-for-profit think tank that works to reduce global poverty and inequality by encouraging policy change in the United States and other rich countries through rigorous research and active engagement with the policy community. The organization's Web site has a lot of reports about and analysis of poverty.

Feeding America
35 East Wacker Dr., Ste. 2000
Chicago, IL 60601
(800) 771-2303
Web site: http://feedingamerica.org

Each year the Feeding America network provides food assistance to more than 25 million low-income people facing hunger in the United States, including more than 9 million children and nearly 3 million seniors. Feeding America's Web site provides information on how to become involved in the organization's network of more than two hundred food banks serving all fifty states, the District of Columbia, and Puerto Rico.

Food First/Institute for Food and Development Policy
398 Sixtieth St.
Oakland, CA 94618
(510) 654-4400
Web site: www.foodfirst.org

The Institute for Food and Development Policy/Food First attempts to influence opinion and policy by analyzing the root causes of global hunger, poverty, and ecological degradation and developing solutions in partnership with movements working for social change. The organization's searchable database has a wealth of information on hunger and poverty.

Heritage Foundation
214 Massachusetts Ave. NE
Washington, DC 20002-4999
(202) 546-4400
e-mail: info@heritage.org
Web site: www.heritage.org

The Heritage Foundation is a conservative think tank that promotes public policy based on limited government and individual freedom. The organization's Web site has a searchable database that includes articles about poverty and welfare.

Hoover Institution
434 Galvez Mall
Stanford University
Stanford, CA 94305-6010

(650) 723-1754 or toll free (877) 466-8374
e-mail: horaney@hoover.stanford.edu
Web site: www.hoover.org

The Hoover Institution on War, Revolution and Peace is a public policy research center devoted to advanced study of politics, economics, and political economy—both domestic and foreign—as well as international affairs. The searchable database on Hoover's Web site contains research and reports on poverty and issues related thereto.

Meals on Wheels Association of America
203 S. Union St.
Alexandria, VA 22314
(703) 548-5558
e-mail: mowaa@mowaa.org
Web site: www.mowaa.org

Meals on Wheels represents member groups that provide home-delivered meal services to people who are elderly, homebound, disabled, frail, or at risk. It also gives cash grants to local senior meal programs throughout the country to assist in providing meals and other nutrition services. The organization's Web site provides information on how to become involved in such programs in your community.

Oxfam International
226 Causeway St., 5th Fl.
Boston, MA 02114-2206
(617) 482-1211
e-mail: info@oxfamamerica.org

Oxfam works to fight poverty throughout the world. The organization's Web site provides policy papers on issues related to hunger and also provides opportunities to aid in the fight against poverty.

The Roundtable on Religion and Social Welfare Policy
Nelson A. Rockefeller Institute of Government
411 State St.
Albany, NY 12203
(518) 443-5041
e-mail: rndtbl@rockinst.org
Web site: www.religionandsocialpolicy.org

The Roundtable on Religion and Social Welfare Policy's mission is to engage and inform government, religious, and civic leaders about the role of faith-based organizations in our social welfare system by means of nonpartisan, evidence-based discussions on the potential and pitfalls of such involvement. Roundtable's searchable database contains many articles and reports about poverty and the role of faith-based institutions in addressing poverty.

U.S. African Development Foundation
1400 I St. NW, Ste. 1000
Washington, DC 20005-2248
(202) 673-3916
Web site: www.adf.gov

U.S. African Development Foundation (USADF) was established by Congress in 1980 as an independent public corporation with a mandate to promote the participation of Africans in the economic and social development of their countries. For more than twenty-five years, USADF has helped grassroots groups and individuals in Africa help themselves by providing the resources they need to advance their own efforts to promote economic and social development. The country portfolio reports summarize the successful programs funded by the organization throughout Africa.

For Further Reading

Books

Arrighi, Barbara A., and David J. Maume, eds. *Child Poverty in America Today*. Westport, CT: Praeger, 2007.

Beaudoin, Steven M. *Poverty in World History*. New York: Routledge, 2007.

Collier, Paul. *The Bottom Billion: Why the Poorest Countries Are Failing and What Can Be Done About It*. New York: Oxford University Press, 2007.

Daly, Lew. *God and the Welfare State*. Somerville, MA: Boston Review, 2006.

DiFazio, William. *Ordinary Poverty: A Little Food and Cold Storage*. Philadelphia: Temple University Press, 2006.

Dumochel, J. Robert. *Government Assistance Almanac 2006–2007: The Guide to Federal Domestic Financial and Other Programs*. Detroit, MI: Omnigraphics, 2006.

Fan, Shenggen, ed., *Public Expenditures, Growth, and Poverty: Lessons from Developing Countries*. Baltimore: Johns Hopkins University Press, 2008.

Moreno-Dodson, Blanca, and Quentin Wodon, eds. *Public Finance for Poverty Reduction: Concepts and Case Studies from Africa and Latin America*. Washington, DC: World Bank, 2008.

Newman, Katherine S., and Victor Tan. *The Missing Class: Portraits of the Near Poor in America*. Boston: Beacon, 2007.

Ruben, R., J. Pender, and A. Kuyvenhoven, eds. *Sustainable Poverty Reduction in Less-Favoured Areas*. Cambridge, MA: CABI, 2007.

Sachs, Jeffrey. *The End of Poverty: Economic Possibilities for Our Time*. New York: Penguin, 2005.

Sticker, Frank. *Why America Lost the War on Poverty—and How to Win It*. Chapel Hill: University of North Carolina Press, 2007.

Vollman, William T. *Poor People*. New York: Ecco, 2007.

Wankel, Charles, ed. *Alleviating Poverty Through Business Strategy.* New York: Palgrave Macmillan, 2008.

Periodicals

Atkinson, Dan. "Eat the Rich, Not the Well-Off," *The Mail on Sunday* (London), August 10, 2008.

Bevan, Judi. "Business Only Thrives When Society Thrives," *Spectator*, October 11, 2008.

Boyd-Zaharias, Jayne, and Helen Pate-Bain. "Class Matters—in and Out of School: Closing Gaps Requires Attention to Issues of Race and Poverty," *Phi Delta Kappan*, September 1, 2008.

Brooks, Steve. "The Cost of Failing to Halt Poverty Is Too Great," *Western Mail* (Cardiff, Wales), September 25, 2008.

Clarke, George R. G., Lixin Colin Xu, and Heng-fu Zou. "Finance and Income Inequality: What Do the Data Tell Us?" *Southern Economic Journal*, January 1, 2006.

Collins, Chuck. "A Problem of Riches: How the Growing Gap Between the Very Wealthy and Everyone Else Is Destroying Our Society from Within," *Sojourners Magazine*, September 1, 2008.

Dealey, Sam. "Class Warfare and the Hard-Working Wealthy," *U.S. News & World Report*, September 2, 2008.

Dickter, Adam. "Does New Poverty Push Have Teeth?" *New York Jewish Week*, August 29, 2008.

Doyle, Leonard. "American Inequality Highlighted by 30-Year Gap in Life Expectancy," *Rachel's Democracy & Health News*, July 24, 2008.

Drucker, Jesse. "America's Richest 1% See Income Share Rise," *Deseret News* (Salt Lake City), July 24, 2008.

Economist. "L-Shaped Poverty Lines; The Legacy of Depression (Lessons from Japan on the Trauma of Economic Crisis)," October 18, 2008.

Entwistle, Jim. "Figures Reveal Child Poverty Hardships," *Northern Echo*, September 30, 2008.

Fletcher, Michael A. "Bush's Poverty Talk Is Now All but Silent; Aiding Poor Was Brief Priority After Katrina," *Washington Post*, July 20, 2006.

Foley, Stephen. "History Lessons," *Independent* (London), October 10, 2008.

Garrett, Thomas A. "U.S. Income Inequality: It's Not So Bad," *Regional Economist*, October 1, 2008.

Gavin, Robert. "Income Chasm Widening in State; Only the Top Earners Gaining, Study Finds," *Boston Globe*, August 15, 2008.

Geller, Adam. "Ordinary Joes Have Mixed Feelings on Wealth," *AP Worldstream*, October 26, 2008.

Grumm, Christine. "Help Eliminate Poverty—Invest in Women," *Record* (Bergen County, NJ), October 22, 2008.

Gurriaran, Jose Antonio. "Spain: Protesters Criticize Aid to Banks Amid Growing Poverty," Inter Press Service English News Wire, October 20, 2008.

Hartevelt, John. "Income Gap Doubles Between Uneducated and Qualified," *The Press*, September 29, 2008.

Holzer, Harry J. "Child Poverty in the U.S.: It Would Be Less Costly to Eliminate than to Tolerate Poverty," *CCPA Monitor*, June 1, 2007.

Inskeep, Steve. "Income Rising for U.S. Middle Class," *NPR Morning Edition*, August 29, 2008.

Jackson, Derrick Z. "Politely Declining to Touch the Income Gap," *Boston Globe*, August 19, 2008.

Jeffrey, Terrence P. "Best Poverty Predictor: Family Status, Not Race," *Human Events*, September 26, 2005.

Kiplinger, Knight. "Does Charity Begin at Home or Abroad?" *Kiplinger's Personal Finance Magazine*, September 1, 2008.

Kokaz, Nancy. "Poverty and Global Justice," *Ethics & International Affairs*, September 1, 2007.

Krishna, Anirudh. "Reversal of Fortune: Why Preventing Poverty Beats Curing It," *Foreign Policy*, May 1, 2006.

Krugman, Paul. "Poverty Is Poison. Poor in the U.S. Today Are Outcasts in Their Own Country," *CCPA Monitor*, May 1, 2008.

Lee, B.J. "A Social 'Time Bomb'; Behind the Facade: Income Inequality Is a Growing Problem," *Newsweek International*, January 23, 2006.

Lobe, Jim. "Economy: Rich Countries Have Wider Gulf Between Rich, Poor," Inter Press Service English News Wire, October 22, 2008.

Mackay, Neil. "Poverty: The Damning Facts," *Sunday Herald*, February 25, 2007.

McVeigh, Karen. "British Child Poverty Rate Doubles," *Scotsman*, March 2, 2005.

Morial, Marc H. "Put Poverty on National Agenda," *New Pittsburgh Courier*, September 27, 2006.

O'Neill, Jim. "As the Poor Get Rich, We'll Get Richer Too," *Sunday Telegraph* (London), July 13, 2008.

Pearlstein, Steve. "Our Inequality of Outcomes," *Washington Post*, August 27, 2008.

PR News Wire. "St. Louis Fed Study Argues U.S. Income Inequality Is Not So Bad," October 6, 2008.

Quintero, Fernando. "Poverty Rate in Colorado Rises to 10.6 Percent; U.S. Figure Dips," *Rocky Mountain News*, August 29, 2007.

Raphael, Dennis. "Poverty and the Economic System: Is Poverty Maintained Because It Helps Keep Wages Down?" *CCPA Monitor*, March 1, 2007.

Saunders, Peter. "A Valuable Contribution to Research and Policy: Reviewing Four Decades of Australian Poverty Research," *Australian Journal of Social Issues*, September 22, 2005.

———. "What Is Poverty?" *Quadrant*, September 1, 2005.

Sicchia, Suzanne R., and Heather Maclean. "Globalization, Poverty and Women's Health: Mapping the Connections," *Canadian Journal of Public Health*, January 1, 2006.

Stark, Pete. "My Word: A Call to End Poverty," *Oakland Tribune*, September 5, 2008.

Swinnerton, Sally. "Living in Poverty and Its Effects on Health," *Contemporary Nurse*, July 1, 2006.

US Fed News Service. "Household Income Rises, Poverty Rate Unchanged, Number of Uninsured Down," August 26, 2008.

Valente, Marcela. "Argentina: Groups Create New Resolve to Battle Poverty," Inter Press Service English News Wire, October 27, 2008.

Wartzman, Rick. "The Joneses and the Joads," *Post-Tribune* (IN), September 21, 2008.

Watts, Rob. "The Poverty of Poverty: The 'Poverty Wars' and the Strange Case of Saunders vs. Saunders Are the Worst Way for Progressives to Look at Inequality in Australia. No Wonder the Neo-cons Like It So Much," *Arena Magazine*, August 1, 2005.

Wilby, Peter. "Inequality Kills," *Rachel's Democracy & Health News*, September 4, 2008.

Williams, Walter. "Our Welfare State Has People Stealing from Each Other," *Deseret News* (Salt Lake City), August 6, 2008.

Williams, Walter E. "Redistributing Income Is Equal to Theft," *Columbia (MO) Daily Tribune*, August 10, 2008.

Wyss, Giulia. "What Is Poverty?" *Earth Focus One Planet—One Community*, September 22, 2006.

Yesudian, C.A.K. "Poverty Alleviation Programmes in India: A Social Audit," *Indian Journal of Medical Research*, October 1, 2007.

Yngwe, Monica Aberg. "Poverty and Social Exclusion in Britain: The Millennium Survey," *Health Sociology Review*, October 1, 2007.

Web Sites

Global Call to Action Against Poverty (www.whitehand.org). This site highlights the work of different countries involved in the Millennium Campaign to fight poverty worldwide.

Heifer Project International (www.heifer.org). The Heifer Project combats hunger, alleviates poverty, and restores the environment by providing appropriate livestock, training, and related services to small-scale farmers worldwide. Heifer Project's key concept is that each recipient must pass on to others some of the offspring of the farm animals they receive.

International Food Policy Research Institute (www.ifpri.org). The institute identifies and analyzes policies to promote sustainable food production to meet the needs of those living in the developing world.

Millenium Campaign (www.milleniumcampaign.org). This site describes the progress countries have made in reducing extreme poverty. The Web site, maintained by the United Nations, provides regional profiles and educates the public about various campaigns to eradicate poverty.

Index

Picture Credits

Maury Aaseng, 13, 22, 29, 36, 41, 46, 52, 57, 64–65, 72, 77, 88, 95, 103, 111, 120, 125

AP Images, 30, 107, 112, 119

© Bill Bachmann/Alamy, 85

James Edward Bates/MCT/Landov, 80

© Steve Bloom Images/Alamy, 42

© Bubbles Photolibrary/Alamy, 70

Chip East/Reuters/Landov, 67

Robert Galbraith/Reuters/Landov, 37

Marko Georgiev/Getty Images, 51

© PHOTOTAKE Inc./Alamy, 78

© Prisma/SuperStock, 16

© Public Record Office/HIP/The Image Works, 97

© SuperStock, Inc./SuperStock, 10, 24

© Visions of America, LLC/Alamy, 47

Max Whittaker/Getty Images, 49

Image copyright Daniel Wiedemann, 2009. Used under license from Shutterstock.com, 59

Alex Wong/Getty Images for *Meet the Press,* 128